D1449692

the love of the samurai

the love of the samurai

a thousand years
of Japanese homosexuality

TSUNEO WATANABE & JUN'ICHI IWATA

Translated by D. R. Roberts

English edition first published November 1989 by
GMP Publishers Ltd, P O Box 247, London N17 9QR.
World copyright ©1987 Tsuneo Watanabe and Juni'chi Iwata.
Translation world copyright © 1989 D. R. Roberts/Triangle
Translations Ltd.

Distributed in North America by Alyson Publications Inc.,
40 Plympton St, Boston, MA 02118, U S A.

British Library Cataloguing in Publication Data

Watanabe, Tsuneo
    Love of the Samurai.
    1. Homosexuality. History
    I. Title   II. Iwata, Juni'chi   III. Voie des Éphèbes
    English
    306.7'66'0952

    ISBN 0-85449-115-5

Printed and bound in the European Community by
Nørhaven A/S, Denmark

Contents

Illustrations

In this book there is reproduced in its entirety a *shunga* erotic roll-painting, comprising ten scenes of homosexual love. The painting is done upon silk 27.3cm in depth. It is by Choshun, and dates from the beginning of the 18th century (at the end of the Genroku period).

All the images are intended to illustrate the varieties of homosexual behaviour. The only woman is shown behind a screen (Plate V). The youth playing the *shamisen* (the Japanese guitar) in Plate I is perhaps a *kagema* (male courtesan, see Chapter IV/2); the one carrying two swords in Plate VIII is a young samurai. As regards the other youths, it is difficult to attribute a precise social position.

Miyakawa (or Hishigawa) Choshun is a well-known painter of *ukiyo-e*. It should be noted that this type of *shunga* roll-painting was always produced in response to a commission by a rich patron. This is the first time that these magnificent works have been published 'uncensored', by courtesy of Dr Richard Lane.

In addition to the painted roll, there are a number of black-and-white illustrations.

Texts by Jun'ichi Iwata

Four essays by Jun'ichi Iwata are included in this volume. They are taken from *Considerations on Japanese Homosexuality* (*Honcho danshoku ko*), published from 1930 to 1933. The translation is literal. In addition to the notes, I have added some explanatory words within brackets. I thank Mr Sadao Iwata, the author's son, for having allowed us to publish these texts.

Proper names

For historical proper names before the Meiji restoration, the name which plays the part of the Western forename is placed in the Japanese fashion, that is to say, after the family name. For modern writers, however, the Western usage has been adopted, as for Yukio Mishima, Taruho Inagaki, etc.

Japanese words

When Japanese words have been used, they are generally printed in italic, with the exception of names of persons and places, and of certain words already familiar in the West, such as 'samurai'. When they appear for the first time, I have tried to give a translation. Where titles are quoted, they have been sometimes left in Japanese when a translation did not seem useful.

Foreword

People in the West are very little aware that there once existed in Japan a cultural tradition of homosexuality comparable to that of ancient Greece. Pederasty in its original sense, the love of an adult male for an adolescent boy, was not at all the object of prohibition until the period of modernisation and industrialisation in the 19th and 20th centuries. It is especially in the 16th, 17th and 18th centuries that it flourished greatly under the rule of the samurai, in a period when the traditional civilisation of Japan reached its perfection. This homosexual love was termed *shudo* (an abbreviation of *wakashu-do*, the way – *do* – of the ephebe, *wakashu*). Far from being condemned, it was considered a passion more noble and more gracious than heterosexuality. It was encouraged, especially within the samurai class; it was considered useful to boys in teaching them virtue, honesty and the appreciation of beauty, while the love of women was often devalued for its so-called 'feminising' effect. A great part of the historical and fictional literature was devoted to praise of the beauty and valour of boys faithful to *shudo*. We find in Jun'ichi Iwata's bibliography of Japanese homosexuality[1] 457 titles from the 17th and 18th centuries. Here is a true corpus of 'erotic pedagogy'.

The rapid decline of *shudo* started with westernisation, from the beginning of the Meiji restoration (1868) onward. In Japan, the process of modernisation was at the same time a rejection and forgetting of this cultural tradition. Around 1910, at the end of the industrial revolution, homosexuality had already disappeared from social visibility. Today, the Japanese only speak of it as a deficiency or a sexual anomaly. An anti-homosexual society has been established, as it has been in Europe.

This is why *shudo*, one of the flowers of Japanese culture, remains unknown in Western countries. Modern writers and historians dissimulate and hide this tradition from foreigners, as they do from Japanese themselves, regarding it as an ancient dishonour. They consider it to be a perversity of morals peculiar to the Japanese ancien régime; they look on it as one of the signs of the 'underdevelopment' of Japanese society. 'Let us love young girls; the Europeans so greatly esteem the love of women,' became the motto of the young poets of the beginning of the 20th century. Homosexual elements have been abandoned, neglected and finally forgotten not only in modern literature and in contemporary life, but also in those traditional art-forms that have survived until today. The *no* theatre, a masked drama comparable to the theatre of ancient Greece, has completely lost its erotic significance as the homosexual theatre of the middle ages. *Kabuki*, a style of theatre still popular today, happily retains the art of the *oyama* (or *on'nagata*), the male actor who plays female roles, but the *oyama* have to hide their homosexuality on the stage and in their private lives. Many plays and scenes showing homosexual relations are no longer performed, on the pretext that they would no longer be to the taste of the contemporary audience. Today, most Japanese, including the so-called 'cultivated', know nothing of the place of *shudo* in the history of Japan. There are some, even, who say: 'The Western vice that we Japanese have never known is invading our country!'

Paradoxically, indeed, the taboo against homosexuality is breaking down and becoming steadily weaker amongst those Westerners whose admiration of heterosexuality was so important to the young Japanese poets. During this century, Japanese and Western attitudes towards homosexuality have been reversed. We now believe the time has come to tell the truth to both Westerners and Japanese alike: that at the time of their greatest glory, the traditional Japanese arts of *no* and *kabuki* were homosexual theatres often linked to prostitution; that what was called the flower of the samurai spirit and formed the real basis of the samurai aesthetic was this *shudo*, the love of young men, and its accompanying ethical and aesthetic codes; and that it is impossible to understand the traditional civilisation of Japan without taking it into account, in the same way as it would be absurd to study Greek art without any understanding of *paiderastia*.

This book was conceived during my first visit to the Louvre. I had been impressed, in the history of Western art, by the loss of the aesthetic function of the male body, and the complete replacement of male nudes by female from the 16th to the 18th centuries. Modernisation resulted in beauty being taken over by women! I could also see a profound relationship between this process and the taboo on homosexuality. I had already thought, for many years, that what was really important in homosexuality was not just sexuality but aesthetics: the admiration for youthful beauty expressed in Greek art was not in some way a consequence of the institution of pederasty. On the contrary, the aesthetic attitude towards the bodies of young men was the basis of the homosexuality of this period. In a society where an aesthetic attitude toward the male body is repressed, homosexuality is repressed as well.

One can see this relationship more easily in Japanese history than in European.

In Japan, the decline of the homosexual tradition was strictly parallel to beauty being taken over by women. It was not due to the Christian taboo against 'sodomy', because Christianity as such had no important role in the modernisation of Japanese society. What was fatal to the cultural tradition of homosexuality was rather the decay of the samurai spirit called *bushido*, the 'way of the samurai', which resulted from the establishment of modern society. In fact, this *bushido* was not only a code of honour for the samurai, but also an aesthetic code, and not for the samurai alone but for all men. When *bushido* died, the masculine aesthetic lost its own norm, and through this *shudo* shared the fate of the samurai society. This is the thesis explored in this book.

Having returned to Japan, impelled by the impression made upon me by the Louvre, I wrote an article in Japanese on the relation between modern society and the contemporary anti-homosexual attitude.[2] As this article was badly received by the Japanese (perhaps because of the ideological absence of interest in the problem of sexual minorities), I rewrote it in French.[3] It was in this way that Michel Bon of Éditions Trismégiste, himself the author of works on sexuality which were already familiar to me, came to give me the opportunity to publish this book.[4] How extraordinary to write my first book on Japanese homosexuality in French! During the last three decades there have been few systematic works on this subject, even in Japan. I am not myself a historian, but a psychologist. This is why I have included in this volume excerpts from essays by Jun'ichi Iwata, an ethnologist and historian of Japanese literature. He remains the greatest scholar of the history of Japanese homosexuality, despite having died unknown in 194 5, one year before my own birth. His work was not welcomed: which shows our total forgetfulness of the cultural tradition of homosexuality in Japanese society.

I would like to thank particularly my French publisher, Michel Bon, who patiently corrected my manuscript and has shown himself a true collaborator. This book is based upon an extensive documentation, and in addition to the works cited in the notes at the end of each chapter, mention must be made of four works in Japanese which refer to the general history of Japanese homosexuality:
* Letters of Kumagusu Minakata to Jun'ichi Iwata (in the *Collected Works of Kumagusu Minakata*, vol. 9, Heibon-sha, 1973).
* *The Complete History of the Japanese Theatre*, by Shigetoshi Kawatake, Iwanami Shoten, 1959.
* *The History of the Homosexual Theatre*, by Masaki Domoto, Shuppan-sha, 1973.
* *Research on Homosexual Literature*, by Kazuyoshi Mori, University of Kochi dissertation, 1982.

This work has been made possible by the help of many people. I should like to express my gratitude to Mr Sadao Iwata, son of Jun'ichi Iwata, who allowed me to translate the texts of his father, now dead; to Dr Richard Lane, a specialist in *ukiyo-e* prints, who provided the wonderful colour photographs; to Professor Jack Pernot of the Franco-Japanese Institute at Kansai and to Professor Kiyoshi Matsuda of the University of Kyoto who both have often advised me on my French.

the love of the samurai

Woman

Adolescent Boy

I. Jesuit Missionaries Against the Sin of Sodom

1. Francis Xavier finds the 'sin of Sodom' everywhere in Japan

In the spring of 1541, Francis Xavier, the first Jesuit missionary to the East, took ship at Lisbon. Seven years previously, in the subterranean chapel of Montmartre, the young Francis, with six other young friends under the leadership of Ignatius Loyola, had taken the triple vows of poverty, chastity and obedience. In the years that followed, their Society had made itself famous by its activities in Italy. It was because of this that King John III of Portugal had asked Loyola to send members of his Society to proclaim the Gospel in Portugal's extensive Eastern colonies. Appointed a papal Nuncio, full of enthusiasm for a mission to India of which he had dreamed for many years, Xavier arrived in Goa, capital of Portuguese India, in May 1542. The Society's famed activity in the Orient had begun.

A short time later, three shipwrecked Portuguese landed on a Japanese island, and became the first Europeans to arrive in Japan. These merchants were well received, and they taught the inhabitants the use of the arquebus, whose manner of construction was soon to become known throughout the Nippon archipelago;[1] this was to be the decisive weapon in the period of civil war which Japanese historians call *sengoku jidai*, 'the period of struggle between the provinces' (1490-1600). Returning to Macao in China, and then to Goa, the Portuguese travellers told stories about this marvellous land, already spoken of by Marco Polo, who had called it Chipango. The inhabitants, they said, were polite and extremely intelligent, with a highly developed sense of honour; they lived under a regime which seemed very close to Europe's feudal system. And so it was that from 1547 the Portuguese captains landed one after another in this Chipango, and the great lords (*daimyo*) of Kyushu, the great southern island of the archipelago, for their part, welcomed these 'barbarians from the South', hoping to consolidate their power by doing business with them.

It was just at this time that Yajiro, an inhabitant of a southern province of Kyushu, Satsuma, left his country aboard a Portuguese ship, having committed a crime. Advised by his kindly captain, Jorge Alvares, the refugee decided to go to Malacca to see the priests and to ask them to 'wash his crime away'. On receiving this unexpected young Japanese visitor, Francis Xavier, who was then in Malacca, became very interested in this land newly opened up to Europeans. Yajiro spoke a little Portuguese, and told the missionary 'about the characteristics of Japan, about the knowledge, culture and intelligence of the inhabitants, about their great need of and readiness for the introduction of our holy Catholic faith.'[2] Francis Xavier immediately decided to put off any other projects so as to be able to go to Japan. He returned to Goa and entered Yajiro at the College of St Paul. In April 1549, Francis Xavier, Father Como de Torres and Brother Juan Fernandez embarked at Goa, together with Yajiro, now baptised with the name Paul. So began the tragic story of the Jesuit apostolate in the Nippon empire.

The little band arrived in Kagoshima, the capital of Satsuma, on 15th August. The lord Shimazu Takahiza (whom the missionaries called 'the king of Satsuma') gave them a good welcome, hoping to engage in trade, and 150 Japanese were baptised in ten months. (This number of converts is quite high, considering the linguistic difficulties faced by the missionaries.) 'The Japanese are the best of the peoples discovered up to now,' wrote Francis Xavier to his companions remaining at Goa, immediately after his arrival in Kagoshima, 'and it seems to me that there will not be another to better them, among the infidels.'[3]

One thing, however, made the missionary angry: 'There are bonzes who love the sin abhorred by nature; they admit it themselves; they never deny it,' he writes in the same letter. 'Nobody, neither man nor woman, young nor old, regards this sin as abnormal or abominable; this sin is well known among the bonzes, and is even a widespread custom amongst them... The bonzes lodge many young sons of samurai within their monastery, and commit this crime with these boys whom they teach reading and writing. The public, even if it does not find it desirable, does not at all consider it outrageous, for it has been the custom for a long time already'.[4]

After ten months' apostolate at Satsuma, Xavier left Kagoshima and set out for Kyoto, so as to ask audience of the supreme sovereign of the empire. When he and his companions, Fernandez and two Japanese converts, arrived at Hakata (today Fukuoka), they visited a large Zen monastery, 'where the bonzes do not believe in anything but this earthly life. And amongst them the abominable vice against nature is so popular that they practise it without any feeling of shame. They have many young boys with whom they commit wicked deeds.[5] The bonzes welcomed the missionaries, believing them to be monks from Tenjiku (the old Japanese name for India), the cradle of Buddhism. 'Just the same, the father loudly condemned the superior and the other monks for committing, shamelessly, such an odious and abominable crime.' The bonzes were greatly surprised; some laughed, while others were reduced to silence. 'And the father left them and went without another word.'[5]

The sin of Sodom was equally widespread among the samurai. Xavier and his companions then arrived at Yamaguchi, whose 'king', Ouchi Yoshitaka (1507-51), was then a prosperous and powerful *daimyo*. The lord welcomed them warmly, and said that he would like to hear the new doctrine of the *kirishitan* (the Japanese mispronunciation of the Latin 'christianus'). Fernandez read in a loud voice from a notebook in which were translated into Japanese the account of the Creation and the Ten Commandments. 'Having touched on the sin of idolatry and on the other faults committed by the Japanese, he arrived at the sin of Sodom, which he described as something so abominable that it is more unclean than the pig and more low than the dog and other animals without reason.[5] Yoshitaka then seemed to be angered, and made a sign for them to go out. 'But the king made not a word of reply, and Fernandez believed that he would order them to be killed'.[5]

Despite Fernandez' fears, the city of Yamaguchi remained for some years the centre of the apostolate in Japan, while Kyoto was almost in ruins as a result of the civil war. Satisfied by the numerous wonderful presents from abroad, the great lord finally gave the Jesuits permission to preach freely. The three great vices of the Japanese chiefly condemned by the father were: abortion and infanticide (which were frequent amongst poor peasants), idolatry, and finally, 'the abominable sin'. The lord simply ignored it when the missionaries spoke like this in the streets, although, at his first interview, it had made him angry.

In 1551, Xavier went to the province of Bungo (today Oita), where the Society found a young lord very favourable to their cause. This great lord, Otomo Yoshikata (1530-87), known today under the name of Otomo Sorin, later became one of the most powerful *kirishitan daimyo* (Christian lords). He offered the missionaries land on which to build a college, but nonetheless hesitated to be baptised himself. The principal reason for this hesitation, according to a letter of Father Belchoir, was that he had 'fallen into those sins which he must abandon if he wishes to become Christian, as he himself recognises very well.'[6] Here is an allusion to the sin of Sodom which we can recognise without difficulty, because the habit of loving young pages (*o-kosho*) was very popular among the nobles at this time. It is said that in 1576 Sorin was finally baptised in the name of Francis. I can't help but suspect that he did not, however, completely abandon his 'vice'.

At the end of 1551, Francis Xavier left Japan with the intention of continuing his mission in China, but on 2 December 1552 he died on an island off Macao, at the age of forty-six. The saint valued the Japanese above all other Asiatic nations. He even wrote that, 'Among the peoples discovered in this region, it will doubtless only be to the Japanese that Christianity may be permanently communicated.'[4] We see his prediction falsified, however, with the great persecution that started in 1597. What was the origin of this miscalculation? Without any experience of Kyoto, which was both the political capital and the centre of Buddhism, Xavier underestimated, it seems to me, the influence of the Buddhist monks. After Father Gaspard Vilela was sent to Kyoto in 1559, the Society extended its field of operations to Kinai (ten provinces around the capital). This meant the beginning of the real struggle against Buddhist influence. We can suppose that the 'abominable vice' was one of the serious points of contention, despite the fact that the Jesuit documents rarely make direct reference to it, doubtless because it was so abominable in nature that one could not speak its name.

2. Christianity and homosexuality

Nobunaga, great captain, homosexual, protector of missionaries
Before going to Kyoto, Father Vilela went with two Japanese converts to Mount Hiei, a Buddhist centre near the capital, in order to have discussions with the monks there. This meeting did not take place, however, because of the death of the monastery's superior, who had invited him. For the next six years, alone in the capital, constantly changing his lodgings as a result of the disfavour he brought to his landlords, he persevered in his mission, without for all that obtaining a good result; the Buddhist monks in particular made trouble for him. They spread rumours that the *kirishitan bonze* was a devil, that he feasted on human flesh, etc. Eventually his personal safety was guaranteed by the shogun Yoshiteru. In 1565, however, when the latter was killed by some nobles, Vilela together with two other missionaries, among them Louis Frois, were banned from the capital and obliged to seek refuge at Sakai, 'a merchant city like Venice'.

This uneasy situation came to an end when Oda Nobunaga (1534-82), lord of the province of Owari (the area around Nagoya), took possession of the capital with the intention of uniting all the provinces. Unusually for a Japanese of this period, this great warlord 'neglected all kinds of veneration or cult of the Buddhas or of the old gods, and held in contempt the superstitious traditions of the pagans.'[7] For several centuries, many great temples had disposed of thousands of soldier-monks (*so-hei*) and were often involved in politics. The Ikko sect in particular organised peasant armies and fought against the great noblemen in many provinces. Greatly irritated by these Buddhist powers, Nobunaga attacked Mount Hiei, burnt the precious buildings and killed 1,200 monks; this caused universal consternation, as the sanctuary was highly revered. On the other hand, he favoured the missionaries, and offered them land beside his castle to build a church and a college. And so, during his fourteen years of power, the movement of the *kirishitan* made astonishing progress. In 1579, the Society sent Mgr Alessandro Valegnani (1537-1606) to Japan as 'visitator', and he was welcomed by Nobunaga. After his tour of inspection in Japan, Valegnani sent four Japanese boys to Rome as representatives of the three *kirishitan daimyo*, of whom Otomo Sorin was one. These young samurai (from 13 to 16 years of age when they left) were received in audience by Gregory XIII, and made a famous tour in Italy, Spain and Portugal (1582-90, see Ill. 1). In 1582, when the visitator returned home, there were 150,000 Japanese converts, including many nobles, and there were 75 missionaries in the field, which was a considerable number for the time.

It was, however, for political reasons that Nobunaga showed favour to the Christians. This great warrior had in reality no inclination to embrace the Christian faith. Indeed he was a person well known to enjoy the pleasure so detested by the Jesuit fathers. There was a remarkable person in the highly eventful life of this captain, a page named Mori Ranmaru, the best known of his young favourites. The service due from these pretty *o-kosho* was not only to receive the attentions of their master, but also to serve him with courage and their sword. For these favourites, the greatest honour would be to fall in battle in order to save their master from peril. The valour and devotion of the young Ranmaru were eloquently praised when he died at the side of his master, who was betrayed and attacked by the army of one of his vassals (Ill. 2). Here is a tie which is due not only to the fidelity proper to the feudal period, but also to eros, and it reminds us of the famous battalion of lovers in the Theban army.

A wicked Buddhist monk, father of the abominable vice
How did Japanese homosexuality appear to the missionaries after Xavier? We find some evidence in a report of visitator Valegnani to the praepostor-general of the Society:

> The first evil we see among them is indulgence in sins of the flesh; this
> we always find among pagans... The gravest of their sins is the most

depraved of carnal desires, so that we may not name it. The young men and their partners, not thinking it serious, do not hide it. They even honour each other for it and speak openly of it. It is not only that the teaching of the bonzes does not regard it as wicked, but that they themselves practise it as a custom entirely natural, and even virtuous... In ancient Japan, I have been told, such a sin did not exist, and all lived in peace under the rule of a single king. But five or six centuries ago, an evil monk put forward the pernicious doctrine nowadays so widespread. What followed were incessant revolt and destruction until our own day. They have been struck by the sword of divine justice, and their crime has been punished.[8]

The evil monk whom Valegnani mentions above was Kobo Daishi, 'the great master Kobo' (774-853), whom certain missionaries spoke of as one of the three great devils, 'Shaka, Amida and Kobo'; Shaka (in Sanskrit Sakya-muni) is the Japanese name of Gautama Buddha; Amitabha is one of the deified Buddhas and the principal deity of the Ikko sect; Kobo, the founder of esoteric Buddhism in Japan, was considered at that time to be the inventor of homosexuality. This person will be described in greater detail in Chapter II/2.

Valegnani continues:

Nevertheless, since Japan has been illuminated by the light of the Gospel, many people have begun to realise how black was their darkness; and the Christians, having listened to reason, avoid and detest these customs.

Some years after the sudden death of Nobunaga, matters began to take a turn for the worse. When Valegnani returned to Japan in 1590 with the four young samurai, he noted that the persecution of the church had already begun. Toyotomi Hideyoshi (1536-98), the successor to Nobunaga, after reuniting the Japanese provinces, ordered European missionaries to go to the port of Hirado, where they had six months to leave Japan altogether. As a Buddhist, Hideyoshi could not shut his eyes to the destruction of the temples in the lands of the Christian lords. All Valegnani's efforts were in vain. It was the end of the golden age of the Japanese church, which in forty years had converted only some 3 per cent of the population. The oppressive policy towards the *kirishitan* was continued by Tokugawa Ieyasu (1542-1614), founder of an extremely stable era of 260 years (the *bakufu* of Tokugawa). He too was a Buddhist, and had an advisory

1. Valegnani and the four young Japanese ambassadors. This print was published at Augsburg in 1586. According to the practice of the church in Japan, the boys have their heads completely shaved. (By permission of the University of Kyoto Library.)

council of monks. The coming of the great persecution of Christians was a sensation, even in Europe. The missionaries, then about 150, were seized and massacred one after the other, and the *kirishitan* were really obliterated with the crushing of a peasant revolt which broke out in Shimabara, a peninsula to the west of Kushu, in 1637. In any event, final victory went to the bonzes. It was just then, with the stabilisation of the political situation and the new prosperity of the great cities, that the custom of homosexuality became popular, under the name of *shudo*, not only in the classes of samurai and monks, but also among the bourgeois class and the townspeople in general. It was indeed then that the Japanese cultural tradition of homosexuality came to its golden age, comparable to that of ancient Greece.

Could a 'Christianised Japan' have successfully destroyed homosexuality?
We may examine the following hypothesis: if Oda Nobunaga had survived the conspiracy, and the Jesuit mission had been able to advance unhindered under the protection of the Oda family,[9] could the Society have successfully eradicated the 'abominable vice' of the Japanese? I believe not, because it is likely that Christianisation by the Society would have changed neither the social organisation of Japan, nor the mentality of the Japanese, even less so that of the samurai. The policy and the principles of propaganda of the Jesuits were not at all incompatible with the spirit of Japanese feudalism of the 16th century. In their work *The Samurai*, R. Storry and W. Forman say:

> When one is studying the psychology and the class organisation of the samurai, it is natural to look for convincing historical parallels in other societies. What comes immediately to mind is the European knight at the high point of feudalism... As far as we know, however, knights and samurai never met, and it is likely that they hardly suspected each other's existence. But four hundred years ago an encounter took place between the samurai and the members of a European 'elite' organised in the fashion of a military caste... The Society of Jesus, the 'cavalry of the Church', won great success in the decades which followed its arrival in the South-West of Japan. Many accounts show us that the Jesuit fathers and the samurai were attracted to each other by feelings of mutual respect.[10]

It is said that converted nobles took up the habit of praying for God's help in victory, as they had previously prayed to Hatchiman Daibosatsu, the Japanese god of war. The conversion did not change the psychology of Japanese warriors.

2. 'The Death of Mori Ranmaru', by the modern graphic artist Mitsuhiro Yoshida. This style with locks growing at the forehead is what was called *mae-gami* or 'front-hair', and regarded as the badge of adolescence. When the young men came of age (18-20 years) this hair was shaved off, as a rite of passage (See Ill. 3). (From *Shosetsu June*, no. 1, 1982, by permission of Mr Yoshida.)

So *bushido*, the samurai spirit, would doubtless have maintained itself in a Catholic Japan, and as we shall see later on, given that *shudo* was intimately linked to it, the latter could have survived as well, though doubtless less openly; in fact, its rapid decline at the beginning of the 20th century has its origin not in the influence of a newly re-imported Christianity, but, as we shall show later on, in the precipitate modernisation of the whole of Japanese society. What was really fatal for the cultural tradition of homosexuality was not the missionaries' struggle against the sin of Sodom, but the Japanese industrial revolution which occurred three centuries later.

The beautiful boy Shiro, last symbol of the movement of Japanese Christians
This is an interesting episode from the Shimabara revolt (1637-38), the last organised resistance of the *kirishitan*. Before the rebellion broke out, a mysterious rumour circulated among the peasants of Shimabara and the island of Amakusa, previously a missionary centre but now harshly governed by anti-Christian nobles: 'Father Marcus predicted, when he left Japan, that 25 years later a wonderful child would appear, and that many miracles would be done. Now the prophecy has been accomplished! An angelic boy is preaching in secret and performs miracles as he goes from one village to another. It is the sixteen-year-old Shiro from Amakusa!'

This mysterious child soon became the leader of the rebels. He said that unbelievers would be punished, and preached every day within the citadel, where were gathered 40,000 persons (peasants with 14,000 women, old people and children) and 40 *ronin* (lordless samurai). After three months' fierce struggle against the imposing forces of the *bakufu*, the citadel fell and all the rebels were massacred. Nothing is known of Shiro, except that he was the son of a *ronin* and that he was beautiful and graceful. Some modern historians consider him to have been the puppet of one faction of the *ronin* in the struggle against the Tokugawa. Nonetheless, the name of Amakusa Shiro remains today in people's memory as a symbol of the movement of *kirishitan*. What interests us here is that he is represented as a *wakashu*, a young boy of 16 years, very beautiful, gracious, dressed in a long-sleeved kimono and with his hair dressed in the *mae-gami* style (hair – *gami*, in front – *mae*) (Ills. 2 and 3).

But indeed, the symbol of *shudo* since the 16th century had been a beautiful *wakashu*. In certain popular novels of our own period, Shiro is loved, even raped by pederastic men. One of the symbols of the *kirishitan* movement which struggled against homosexuality is being absorbed into the Japanese homosexual tradition. A fine irony of history... What, however, really made Shiro appear on the scene was perhaps an older and more fundamental tradition than that of *shudo*. A very

ancient tradition in Japan is the cult of the young boy as a divinity incarnate. This cult, in my view, is at the basis of the tradition of homosexuality in Japan, one of whose manifestations is precisely Amakusa Shiro's appearance as a beautiful *wakashu*. We will study this tradition more closely in Chapter II.

3. The costume of the *wakashu* (centre) in the 17th century. Apart from the difference in hairstyle between the young man and the two adults (the *wakashu*'s servant and a samurai), we see that the young man's sleeves are longer. These long kimono sleeves are called *furi-sode*, and they too were a mark of adolescence. Both young men and young women wore *furi-sode*. (From Ihara Saikaku's 'Glorious tales of homosexuality', 1689, reprinted in *Nihon koten bungaku zenshu*, vol. 39, Shogaku-kan, Tokyo, 1973.)

II: The Love of *Chigo* in the World of the Monks

1. *The myth of the origin of Japanese homosexuality*

(this section is an extract from Juni'chi Iwata)

It is easy to follow in later history the consequences of an event. It is difficult, however, or almost impossible, to succeed in the search for its 'origin'. If we insist on finding this, we will often end up in the world of legends and oral tradition, which takes us far from our own reality: I do not know myself, at the beginning of this search for the origin of Japanese homosexuality, how to escape this kind of absurdity. Nonetheless, even if the traditions we may find in these kinds of account seem to refer to unbelievable events, allow me to treat them provisionally as historical facts, for there might well be something of historical value even in these traditions.

According to popular tradition, Japanese homosexuality began with the monk Kukai, better known by his posthumous title, Kobo Daishi. He returned from China in the first year of the Daido era (AD 806), at the beginning of the Heian period, and it was precisely this, a Chinese custom, that he is said to have introduced with the *Shingon* teachings. It soon became fashionable among certain monks, was then adopted by notable laymen, and finally spread among the people, winning over the whole of Japan. Today, however, we have no means of knowing in what way Kukai was homosexual. Nor are we told in any historical work that it was this great monk who imported and encouraged this foreign custom previously unheard of.

As it concerns this great master, in any case, the vulgar tradition relates not a matter of fact, but the feelings of posterity. It is probable that people attached the name of Kukai to the strange custom of homosexuality; in the same way there were stories told about the wanderings of a mysterious pilgrim who travelled through all the provinces, performing many miracles.[1] These stories about Kobo Daishi, in my view, are simply legends.[2]

31

'It is said that the taste for homosexuality came from the monk Kukai's voyage in China. This custom, however, had doubtless already existed for a long time already, for we find in the *Shoku nihon gi*[3] a paragraph which indicates that in the era of the emperor Koken the prince Doso secretly had relations with his child-servant or *ji-do*.'[4] According to another opinion, it was indeed after Kobo Daishi that libertine bonzes indulged in homosexual relations: this is an article on 'The Origin of Things in Japan', written by Kaibara Koko in the Tenwa era (1681-84). If we examine the *Shoku nihon gi* ourselves, we find in the paragraph in Vol. 20 concerning the first year of the Tenpyo-hoji era of emperor Koken (AD 757), a description of the ministers meeting and discussing the 'disorderly behaviour' of prince Doso: 'The prince, however, has secret relations with a servant-child despite the fact that mourning for the old emperor has not yet ended.'

It seems to me that the author of 'The Origin of Things in Japan', seeing the phrase 'his servant-child', has rashly interpreted it as expressing the beginning of homosexuality. But if we look at the meaning of the word in its total context, we see that this note does not imply homosexuality at all. In fact, the word 'servant-child', in this period, could mean equally a young maidservant or a young page. The other ground for objection to Mr Kaibara is that the author of *Shoku nihon gi*, criticising the 'disorderly behaviour' of the prince, presents as evidence only the conduct noticed above. If we suppose that this 'child' really means a boy, is the prince being condemned for a disorderliness expressed in homosexuality? Does the author mention this fact because homosexuality was detestable and unforgivable or indeed because the custom of homosexuality was still rare at that time?

The context refutes these conjectures. If the 'relations with a servant-child' were of a homosexual nature, why should the author remark on this curious taste of the prince's only in relation to the period of mourning? Prince Doso was probably condemned by his ministers because he made love to his maidservant despite the period of mourning, and not because he practised homosexuality.

Nonetheless, the scholars and literati of the Edo period, in their works, follow without exception the dogma of the 'Origin of Things in Japan'. Even Amano Nobukage,[5] who cites this interpretation in his *Shiojiri*, treats it as truthful. All these erroneous ideas are no doubt due to Mr Kaibara.

In searching for the origin of homosexuality, I ended up arriving at the *Nihon Shoki*,[6] one of the oldest books in Japanese. The point where I was able eventually to stop already belonged to the domain of legend. In the search for documentary sources, I could see no point in going any further. In the paragraph on the first year of the era of the empress Jingu, in Vol. 9,[7] one finds a sin called the sin of *azunai*, 'azunai no tsumi'. This sin is presented, in fact, as the homosexual vice abominated by the gods, like the sin of Sodom in the Old Testament.

It was Shinu no Hafuri and Ama no Hafuri who first committed the sin of *azunai*. Although it was their duty to serve their god, they were *uruwashiki tomo* or 'very intimate friends', who loved each other dearly. When Shinu no Hafuri departed this world after an illness, Ama no Hafuri, left alone, so deeply grieved this death that he ended by killing himself alongside the dead body of his friend. They were buried together in the same grave. Since then, the sun no longer shone at this spot and it was always as dark as the middle of the night. And so it was said that the sin of homosexuality had been abominated by the gods.

Here is an extract from the account:

> The empress went southward and arrived in the province of Ki... then she went to the palace of Shinuno. At that time, it was always dark, as if it were the middle of the night, and it had been so for many days. The people spoke of 'the empress's voyage through perpetual night'. She asked of Toyomimi, an ancestor of the Ki, 'What is the reason for this wonder?' And there was there an old man, who answered the empress, saying, 'I once heard it said that such a wonder is the sign of what is called the sin of *azunai*... it is probably because they buried together the priests of two Shinto temples.' And so she had the villagers questioned by Toyomimi, and one of them told this story: 'Once there were two good friends, Shinu no Hafuri and Ama no Hafuri. When the first died of a sickness, Ama no Hafuri wept greatly and said, "While he was alive, we were very intimate friends. Why should we not have the same grave?" So he killed himself, right next to the dead body. That is why they buried them both in the same tomb. That is the sin concerned, I presume.'
>
> The empress had the tomb in question opened, and saw that it was true. Then she had the two bodies each placed in a new coffin and buried separately in different places. Immediately, the sun began to shine, and the night and day were again divided the one from the other.

This is the first description of homosexuality in all the Japanese chronicles. My researches on the origin of homosexuality have allowed me to go back this far. In this note, the sin of *azunai* is what an old man had once heard spoken of. It concerns a very distant time. The history of Japanese homosexuality begins with a mythic tradition; this ought to be known by those who believe thatthe custom was first disseminated by the monk Kukai, in the ninth century AD.[8]

(end of extract from Jun'ichi Iwata)

2. Two great esoteric masters

From the century of the Jesuit missionaries, let us go back to the ninth century to look for the origin of the cultural tradition of homosexuality. Here too we shall see enthusiastic religious cross the sea despite all difficulties. Two Buddhist monks, Saicho (767-822) and Kukai (774-835), having learnt the new Buddhist doctrines in China, returned to their country to teach them to the Japanese, who, according to them, did not yet know true Buddhism. The first, known by his posthumous name of Dengyo Daishi, 'Great Master of the Propagation of the Teachings', taught his new doctrines at the temple of Enryaku-ji on Mount Hiei, and became the founder of the *Tendai* school. The second, having received the esoteric doctrine at Chang-an, the capital of China, created the shrine of Mount Koya, became the founder of the esoteric school of *Shingon* or the 'true word', and would become the most famous Japanese saint. It is said that their return from China is the most important event in the history of Japanese Buddhism since the sixth century, the time of its introduction.

We can equally say that it is the most notable event in the whole history of the homosexual cultural tradition in Japan.

Master Kobo, pioneer of Japanese homosexuality?
In fact, homosexuality was destined to develop first in the two schools of *Tendai* and *Shingon*, and to spread outwards later. It was Mount Koya particularly, the great centre of the *Shingon* school, which the European missionaries of the 16th century would mention as the centre of homosexuality. Moreover, it was precisely Kukai who was presented to Europeans by the visitator Valegnani as the inventor of the sin of Sodom; Kobo Daishi, or 'Great Master of the Propagation of the True Doctrine', is his posthumous title.

'In the place called Mount Koya, there are many communities of bonzes. Their founder is called Kobo Daishi. To judge by what he has done, this bonze was not a man, but a devil... It is the custom of the Japanese, if they wish to retire from the

34

world, to cut off their hair and enter one of these communities, in the same way as we do when we take the habit of a monk. However, the Japanese who enter there satisfy their own desires, and allow the bodily life to thrive' (Louis Frois: letter of 20 February 1565).

'The people have been terribly deceived by a bonze called Kobo Daishi. I find, according to what has been told me, that he was altogether the devil incarnate. He invented numerous sins, and taught them to the people' (Vilela: letter of 13 August 1561).

The legend which has it that Kobo Daishi invented homosexuality, or imported it from China, was at that time considered to be authentic. In addition, the invention of the *kana*, the Japanese phonetic writing system, was ascribed to him. According to another tradition, this great master is not dead, but remains immobile in his grave. in *samadhi*, and will reappear on earth after 5,670,000,000 years to meet Maitreya, the future Buddha. A host of fabulous deeds are attributed to this brilliant, wonderful, mystical and more than natural man. The son of a provincial noble family, destined for an official career, he was sent to the capital to pursue his studies at the university. He left the town, however, at the age of eighteen, to live as a hermit in the mountains. Without master or adviser, he meditated in an isolated cave, studying the esoteric texts and dreaming of going to China, where there lived, he believed, his true master. Along the supposed course of his journey, 88 pilgrimages were established, which are still very popular today, and I myself, when I was young, spent 41 days doing the journey on foot .

It was when he was 31 that Kukai met in China the true inheritor of Indian esoteric Buddhism. Hardly had he set eyes on the foreign student when the great Chinese master smiled kindly at him and announced in a joyful voice:

> I knew already of your coming, and I have expected you for a long time. I am very happy to see you today. My personal existence on this earth is coming to its end, but I find no one among my disciples capable of receiving the true esoteric teaching. That is why, my son, I will ask you to look after the two mandalas and the texts of the Doctrine... And now go, go, my son, go and spread our teachings in the land of your birth! [9]

Nonetheless, we cannot distinctly recognise any evidence of homosexuality in his biography. The Japanese seem already to have known homosexuality a long time before Kobo Daishi, as Jun'ichi Iwata has shown at the beginning of this chapter. It is probable that later on, when they saw homosexuality thrive in the esoteric monasteries, people considered the saint to be the discoverer, or one might say the patron saint, of these special customs. It is rather with another great religious, Saicho, that we shall be able to find an episode involving homosexuality.

Two great masters and the young Shinpan: a *ménage à trois*?

Saicho was seven years older than Kukai, and after ten years of the hermit's life on Mount Hiei he went to China at the same time as his great contemporary. In 805, he returned to Japan decided on bringing about the victory of the new doctrine he had learnt on Mount Tiandai (Tendai in Japanese), in Zhejiang. Contrary to his own intentions, he was welcomed not for the Tendai teachings, but for the fragmentary knowledge of esoteric doctrine which he had picked up by the way. What interested the emperor and the courtiers of the time were not the teachings of 'salvation', but rather the supernatural effectivity of the esoteric rites. It was therefore natural that he should lose his popularity when Kukai came back one year later as the authentic master of esoteric Buddhism. A sincere enthusiast, Saicho wanted to introduce these true esoteric teachings to his own school, and he sent Kukai his best disciple to be trained. This young monk, Shinpan, preferred to remain with Kukai and did not return to his old master. All Saicho's pleas were in vain. Looking at his letters to Shinpan, Shiba, a modern writer and Kukai's biographer, declares that there is certainly some kind of love in Saicho's feeling for his disciple.[10] Even if it is not a case, here, of *paiderastia* properly speaking – because Shinpan was then more than twenty years of age – it seems certain that this great monk had a strong homosexual tendency, spiritually speaking at least.

After the tragic death of Saicho, the Tendai school zealously introduced the esoteric into its teaching in a bid to compete with Kukai's rival school. Towards the end of the ninth century Mount Hiei thus became the second great centre of esoteric Buddhism.

Master Saicho meets an angelic boy on Mount Hiei

At the same time, a remarkable tradition built up around Saicho. In 785, the young Saicho entered upon the hermit's life on Mount Hiei by taking the five vows of a boddhisattva. One day, as he was making his way through the forest, he met an angelic boy.

'Who are you, mysterious boy?' asked Saicho. The angelic child replied, saying, 'I am really the divine child who rules the world. I am the god of Dosei, also known

4. Chigo Daishi (the child Kukai). (Detail from a painting on silk, 14th c.,
artist unknown.)

as the *deva* of Nissho, the god of Yugyo or the Master Juzen.[11] I assure you that your prayers will be answered.

Saicho worshipped the child and said, 'Oh, my master Juzen, I offer you all my devotion. This mountain is truly sacred and fortunate. In your name, I vow to overcome all lust!'

It was at this spot that Saicho decided to establish the headquarters of his teaching, the temple of Enryaku-ji. And this is why the monks of Mount Hiei admired the *chigo* (young boy) as the incarnation of Master Juzen. They even said, 'First worship the *chigo*, and second, worship Sanno' (tutelary deity of Mount Hiei).

There is another, similar, tradition. On his way back to Japan, Saicho was overtaken in the open sea by a terrible tempest. He prayed, and immediately saw appear upon the waves an angelic boy, who announced his name as 'Father of the Tendai teachings' and stilled the storm.

The gods appear incarnate in the form of angelic boys
What do these mysterious traditions signify? In my opinion, they are represen-tations of a very ancient Japanese cult: 'the gods appear incarnate in the form of angelic boys' (see Ill. 16a). And these legends in turn provide the spiritual basis of homosexuality in the Tendai school, even in all the Buddhist schools. During the following centuries, it was the custom of aristocrats to enter their sons temporarily in the monasteries, sometimes to prepare them for a clerical life, and it was natural that these well brought-up young boys, called *chigo*, should be the object of a sexual love. At the same time, 'because they are gods incarnate', these *chigo* were also the object of worship and spiritual admiration. This contributed to the development of homosexual love, in the same way as the cult of the Virgin seems to have contributed to the evolution of the love of women in medieval Europe. In fact, the dénouement of many '*chigo* stories' written by monks of the 14th and 15th centuries is that a beloved and beautiful *chigo* reveals himself to be a god or boddhisattva incarnate.

Throughout the following centuries (the Heian period), during which there was a great flourishing of aristocratic culture at the court of Heiankyo (the old name of Kyoto), this form of homosexuality steadily developed, above all in the monasteries of the two esoteric schools. Nonetheless, this melancholy monastic love is hardly taken as the principal subject in literary works, at least not until the end of the period. What then pleased the readers best were tales of amorous intrigue at court – heterosexual of course. We have very many tales of love, written particularly by the ladies of the court, of which the most famous is certainly *Genji Monogatari*, the 'Tale of Genji'. It is surprising, however, that even in this Don-Juanesque tale written by a woman, we find a homosexual episode: one evening, Lord Genji, missing his beloved, sleeps with her little brother, a young and pretty boy who very much resembles his sister.[12] This suggests that in the high society of Heiankyo the love of boys was accepted, and tolerated without condemnation. As regards homosexual literature proper, there remain only a certain number of poems written by monks to their beloved *chigo*.

The situation changed in the twelfth century. The ancient aristocracy gave way to the political hegemony of two military clans, the Taira and the Minamoto, from whom would be descended the higher classes of samurai. As for the literary hegemony, it passed from the courtesans and ladies of the court to the Buddhist clergy of the monasteries. So we find among the tales and legends written and collected at this time a certain number of anecdotes and short stories which have the love of *chigo* as their theme. We present here quite a short story, but a fine one, taken from the *Kokonchomon-shu*, a collection of anecdotes put together in the 13th century which contains many stories of homosexuality. It is a true story set in the Ninna-ji, the great abbey of the Shingon school.

3. Love in the monasteries

The lord abbot and his two favourites

The lord abbot of Ninna-ji, who was one of emperor Toba's princes, was much in love with a *chigo* called Senju. A beautiful and affectionate boy, he played the flute well and performed well in fashionable songs. One day, another *chigo* named Mikawa entered the monastery as a novice; he was a good player on the *koto* (the Japanese 13-stringed zither), and also a clever poet. The lord preferred this new favourite to Senju, who, believing himself dishonoured, no longer appeared before his master. One evening, the lord had organised a small dinner, and in the middle of the various entertainments he remembered his old love and sent his servant to look for him, saying, 'Why has Senju not come forward? I would like to hear him sing and play the flute.'

First of all, Senju would not accept his lord's invitation. It was only at the third demand that he appeared. He dressed himself very gracefully: the violet of the long dress was astonishing; yet he seemed altogether sad. Called upon by the guests, the boy sang:

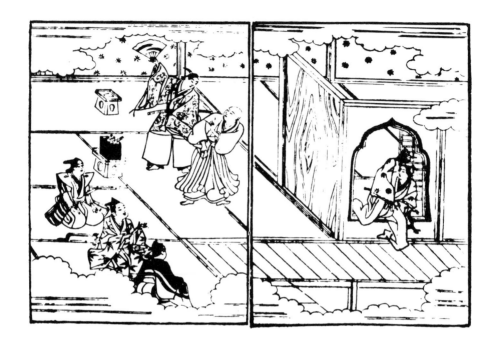

5. 'Senju and Mikawa.' The lord abbot carries Senju in his arms and goes directly to his room. On the right, Mikawa is going to leave the monastery. (Reproduced in *Honcho danshoku ko.*)

What shall I do? I am abandoned
Even by the innumerable ancient Buddhas.
Among the innumerable paradises I find
None where I may be reborn.
Buddha Amida, my last resort,
Though I am such a sinner,
May I be saved by your hand!

He drew attention to the phrase 'I am abandoned', singing it more quietly. All were reduced to tears. The lord, especially, was so moved that he took Senju in his arms and went immediately into his chamber. All the guests spoke of it with great interest throughout the night. The next morning on waking, the lord found a poem written on the screen, in which Mikawa, moved by the transience of human feeling, made his farewells to the abbot. It was heard that he became a monk in a distant temple (Ill. 5).

The tender attentions of a young *chigo* towards his old master

From the beginning of the 14th century there are written true homosexual novels, which the historians call *chigo monogatari* or 'chigo stories'. The most primitive and the most frank of this kind remains as a manuscript, jealously guarded as part of the treasure of the temple of Daigo-ji, a great esoteric monastery. This 'Chigo no soshi' or 'Chigo notebook' contains five tales written on an *emakimono* or roll-painting. Here is one:

At the abbey of Ninna-ji, there was a famous and highly venerated monk. Already very old, he was of incomparable virtue, but he had not for all that renounced the pleasures of boy-love. Around him, then, were always many favourites. The master loved one of them above all, and most often slept with this beautiful young boy. But, already old, all he could manage was 'to rub his arrow between two hills'; penetration was out of the question. This his favourite deplored, and every evening he made himself ready for his dear master.

First he called his servant, the son of his wet-nurse, and got him to 'work with his fingers'. Then he got him to insert an enormous *harikata* (dildo) in his anus. Then he asked him to fill it with *choji*, a kind of vegetable oil, and finally he warmed his pretty bottom over a brazier (Ill. 6).

The servant, devotedly doing such work for the beautiful *chigo*,

41

always got an erection and was unable to prevent himself from masturbating.

As for the old master, he rose very early as a result of his age, and having little to do he used to call his beloved to him in the early hours of the morning. As the *chigo*'s preparation had become perfect, the master succeeded in penetrating without difficulty.

'It is with such affectionate feelings and such tender attentions,' concludes the author, 'that a *chigo* is of incomparable value.'

A long story for an autumn night, or the tragedy of the beautiful Umewaka
There remain to us the eight '*chigo* stories' in the form of novels, all written during the 14th and 15th centuries. We give a resumé of one called '*Aki no yo no naga-monogatari*', or 'Long story for an autumn night'. It is based on the fact that the temple of Mii-dera, the mother-abbey of a sect of the Tendai school, came into conflict with Mount Hiei over a *chigo* of unrivalled beauty:

At the time of the emperor Nijo (1152-6l), there was on Mount Hiei a monk called Keikai. One day he took to the temple of Ishiyama-dera, so as to pray for success in his studies to Kannon Bosatsu, the boddhisattva most worshipped in Japan (in Sanskrit: Avalokiteshvara, in Tibetan: Tchenrezig). During the last night of his stay, sleeping before the statue of Kannon Bosatsu, he saw in his dream an exceptionally beautiful boy. Keikai fell in love with him on the spot, though he remained sceptical of his actual existence. What a surprise for him then, on the way home, to glimpse behind the great gate of the monastery of Mii-dera a beautiful youth who looked like the boy in his dream. He seemed to be about fifteen or sixteen years of age. Keikai was told that the beautiful *chigo* was called Umewaka (literally 'young plum-tree'), and that he was the son of a minister. The monk Keikai took lodgings in this monastery and sent him a love-poem. To his great surprise, he received a poem in reply. After a certain exchange of poetry, Keikai was secretly introduced into Umewaka's rooms. Such was the beauty of the face that Keikai saw by the light of the candle that 'the flowers were envious and the moon jealous. It could not be drawn with a brush, nor described in words...' (Ill. 7).

After a delicious evening, Keikai returned to Mount Hiei. Meanwhile, the passion which he had inspired in the boy became more and more irresistible, and he fled Mii-dera to see his lover. Unfortunately, on the road to Mount Hiei, the boy was kidnapped by a brigand and imprisoned in a distant place. Noticing the disappearance of the beautiful *chigo*, people at Mii-dera said, 'It's them, Keikai and

42

6. Right: the *chigo* warms his bottom at a charcoal fire.
   Left: then he enters his lord's room.
(Reproduced in *Kokubungaku kaishaku to kansho.*)

43

those from Hiei, who have done this,' and they called together two thousand warrior-monks. At this, the people of Hiei lost their temper: they attacked Mii-dera with a hundred thousand warrior-monks, and after a fierce struggle, set fire to the numerous buildings of the abbey.

Umewaka, happily delivered from the brigands by an old man, returned to Mii-dera. Seeing his monastery reduced to ashes, he cried out, 'The fault is mine! I cannot live any longer!' and ended his short life by throwing himself into the water.

Keikai so deeply regretted the death of his beloved that after giving him a loving burial he left Mount Hiei and became a hermit.

As for the monks of Mii-dera, who were sleeping in a little building that had been spared the flames, they dreamt one night that Shiragi Daimyojin, the tutelary deity of the Mii-dera temple, had received the tutelary deity of Mount Hiei as a friend. 'Alas, holy patron,' they cried out in their dream, 'we don't understand at all what you are doing.' Shiragi Daimyojin replied:

'Good and evil are not always the same for men as they are in the law of the Buddha. This catastrophe has been the occasion of the true conversion of Keikai. He will become a religious of great virtue. His name will outlive him. In truth, Umewaka was no other than Kannon Bosatsu of Ishiyama-dera, become flesh so as to allow the conversion of Keikai...'

An esoteric or 'Tantric' basis for homosexual pleasure

Can the desires and passions undisguisedly presented in these stories be regarded as the shame and corruption of religious men? Japanese historians of modern times believe this to be the case, and often claim that homosexuality is a sign of the decadence of Japanese Buddhism.

When, however, we reconsider esoteric Buddhism in its Indian origins, we see that this is not true. What has always been the difference between the esoteric teachings, often called Tantric Buddhism, which flourished in India from the fifth to the eighth centuries AD, and traditional 'exoteric' Buddhism? It is that the secret teachings offer men, all men, the possibility and the means to obtain 'deliverance' (in Sanskrit: *vimoksha*) in this life. Even living, one can become a Buddha! This doctrine has many points of similarity with Tantric Hinduism. The body is not despised, it is respected as a microcosm essentially identical with the macrocosm. There is no more denial of the wishes or desires of the flesh; all beings are 'in essence' pure, and even holy. It is natural therefore that the line between Buddhism and Hinduism becomes ever more unclear, and that by the end of the eighth century Tantric Buddhism had come to regard the sexual act as holy.

7. 'Umewaka and the monk Keikai'. The person on the right is
Umewaka's young servant. (An illustration of the 17th c., reproduced in
Iwata's *Honcho danshoku ko*.)

What was transmitted to both China and Japan was certainly the orthodox esoteric doctrine of the previous centuries, but in the *Rishu-kyo* sutra (in Sanskrit: *Adhyardhar'satika Prajnaparamita*), highly regarded by Kukai, we nonetheless find the following phrases:

> To say that voluptuousness is pure is a truth of the state of boddhisattva. To say that desire is pure is a truth of the state of boddhisattva... to say that physical pleasure is pure is a truth of the state of boddhisattva;
> To say that sounds are pure is a truth of the state of boddhisattva. To say that tastes are pure is a truth of the state of boddhisattva. To say that tangible things are pure is a truth of the state of boddhisattva;
> To say that visual forms are pure is a truth of the state of Boddhisattva;
> And why? It is because all *dharmas*, all creatures, are in essence pure.

How then could the esoteric teachers help arriving at the doctrine that all wishes and desires of the flesh are permitted? In the monasteries, however, they found the traditional injunction to celibacy and prohibition on the love of women. Between a metaphysics and a monastic rule that contradicted each other, what should be done?

The only way out was to love a beautiful boy. In homosexuality, the esoteric monks found a solution faithful at the same time to traditional commandment and to Tantric arcana.

The Buddhist monks' rule of celibacy would be abandoned by the Ikko sect (who worshipped Buddha Amida), which became, from the 15th century, the largest religious denomination. A decree of the *bakufu* of Edo allowed bonzes to marry. In this way, the severity of the sexual prohibitions applying to monks was steadily relaxed. This seems to run in parallel with the process by which the cultural tradition of homosexuality passed gradually from the Buddhist monks into the hands of the ascendant class of samurai.

III: The Love of *Wakashu* in the World of the Samurai

1. History

Adolescent boys in the period of civil wars

The cultural tradition of homosexuality underwent a remarkable transformation in the world of the samurai: the term which designated the object of pederastic love changed from *chigo* (literally: young child) to *wakashu* (literally: young man). This corresponds to a change in the age suitable to be loved: the *chigo* would have been from about ten or eleven to sixteen or seventeen years old; the *wakashu* was now from about thirteen or fourteen to eighteen or nineteen, sometimes even more than twenty years old. There appeared a homosexuality of a military type comparable to that of the Spartans. This kind of pederasty was called *shudo*.

We are now back in the century of the European missionaries, the 16th. We may recall that the Jesuit priests witnessed the ending of the *bakufu* of Muromachi. In 1565 Ashikaga Yoshiteru, the thirteenth shogun, died while being attacked in his palace by the army of one of his generals. The protection the shogun had offered the missionaries now lost its effect and two of the fathers, Gasparo Vilela and Louis Frois, were obliged to flee from Koyoto (see Chapter I).

No Japanese document is as detailed and lively as that of Father Frois; our attention is drawn by one passage in particular:

> A boy of thirteen years of age, the son of a distinguished nobleman called Odachidono, a page to my lord the Shogun, fought so valiantly and with such intrepid spirit that all the rebels started to shout out that he should not be killed, but that he should be taken alive. Nonetheless, seeing his master die, and believing it a great dishonour to survive him, the young boy threw away his sword, and pulling out his dagger, he cut open his throat and then his belly; finally he killed himself by lying down flat with the dagger in his belly.

Frois seems to tell this story without noticing the erotic significance of the young boy's death. Did this 'page to my lord the Shogun' fight and die from simple loyalty, or for honour only? He died, it seems to me, just as much for the tie of love that attached him to his master, as the praiseworthy Ranmaru, twenty years later, also fought and died at the side of Nobunaga his master (Chapter I). Young samurai of this kind, lovers and warriors at the same time, took the place of the gentle and effeminate *chigo* and became the new heroes of homosexual culture in Japan. Father Frois's article, unbeknown to the author himself, tells us that the 16th was already a century of the *shudo* in the proper sense. It is in fact in 1485 that the word *shudo* appears in a document for the first time.

Shudo is an abbreviation of *wakashu-do*, which means the way (*do*) of the youth (*wakashu*), or more literally, the way of young (*waka*) men (*shu*). *Do*, or sometimes *to*, is the Japanese reading of the Chinese ideogram *tao*. Considered by Taoists as the very principle of the universe, it also means the Way by which one reaches awakening, the means by which one becomes conscious of one's true nature. In Japan, every art and every technique can become a Way towards awakening if it requires a long and difficult apprenticeship. We may search for awakening not only by the Way of the Buddha (*Butsu-do*), or by that of the gods (*shin-to*), but also by the Way of the Bow (*kyu-do*) or by that of Suppleness (*ju-do*), or even by that of Tea (*sa-do*) or of Calligraphy (*sho-do*)! In any event, what is suggested by the appearance of the word *shudo* is that the times called for more strength, bravery and independence in the young favourites who previously needed only be gentle, pretty and passive. The 15th and 16th centuries correspond to a long period which brought such troubles as the Japanese had never yet met. In this era of *sengoku* (struggles between provinces), we shall see how the weak Umewakas were little by little replaced by people like the praiseworthy Ranmaru or Shogun Yoshiteru's valiant page (Ill. 6).

The change from the love of *chigo* to *shudo* in the house of the shoguns
In the history of Japanese homosexuality, fashions seem to spread from the top down. It is not at all surprising to meet the first instance of the typical development of the love of *chigo* into *shudo* in the history of the house of the shoguns, the Ashikaga family. The third shogun Ashikaga Yoshimitsu (1358-1408) seems to have remained within the homosexual tradition of the priests and the aristocrats. He especially liked to visit the temples of the different provinces, where he appreciated the music and dancing of the young performers. Not only in the *sarugaku* companies, but also in the *dengaku* or 'rustic dances' (ancestor of *no*) which rivalled the former, and in the *ennen no mai* performances which originated

in monkish amusements, the stars were without exception beautiful young men. Some were invited to court by Yoshimitsu: they pleased him and he granted them favours. The most remarkable was the young Fujikawa, the future Zeami (see Chapter IV/1).

It was however a young samurai, and not an actor, who influenced the life of the fourth shogun Yoshimochi (1368-1427), the son of Yoshimitsu. The young man he liked was called Akamatsu Mochisada, a prince of the Akamatsu family, who had distinguished themselves in the battles which led to the establishment of the *bakufu* of Muromachi and the military government of the Ashikaga.

A fifteenth-century document relates the following:

> In the era of Lord Yoshimochi, Akamatsu Akinori had seven children, of whom the youngest was called Yagoro Mochisada.[1] A very beautiful young man, he was granted three provinces (Harima, Bizen and Mimasaka) simply through the homosexual favours of the lord. Proud of this favour, he conducted himself in such an arbitrary manner that he committed injustices which caused everyone to frown; but no one dared accuse this favourite lover. However, Akamatsu Mitsusuke, chief of the clan of the Akamatsu, considering this a dishonour to the clan, brought many great lords to his side and issued an accusation against Mochisada, who was unable to deny his guilt. Ordered to do so by Lord Yoshimochi, Mochisada killed himself by hara-kiri.

It is said that Yoshimochi died of an illness, full of hatred against Mitsusuke, upon whom he had not found the means to revenge himself. Yoshinori (1394-1441), the sixth shogun, Yoshimochi's younger brother, wished to live only for his homosexual love and finally died of it. At the age of ten, he entered a monastery where he was the beloved of a monk of the Zen sect. On the premature death of Yoshimochi, having laicised himself, he acceded to the post of shogun. From then on he made favourites of his vassals' sons; he often visited the temples, where he looked for young and beautiful performers whom he brought back to his palace and there took advantage of them. He had a passion for the young actor Oto-ami, a nephew of the great Zeami whom he banished, having accused him of refusing his nephew the post of head of the company. Finally he fell to doting on a young man called Akamatsu Sadamura, which was to lead the shogun to his fatal disaster. Sadamura, the nephew of Akamatsu Mochisada, having lost his father early, had lived without lordship. Since the shogun had made him his page, however, 'He received homosexual favour the like of which will not anywhere be found. Lord Yoshinori, desiring to advance this young man to the rank of head of the Akamatsu, sent him a secret message telling him to confiscate three provinces of Akamatsu Mitsusuke and giving them to him.' The rumour came to the ears of Mitsusuke, who, greatly angered, invited the shogun to a banquet one evening and murdered him. This is what is called the Kakitsu affair (the Kakitsu era designates the years 1441 to 1443).

With the next affair, called the Onin civil war (the Onin era designating the years 1467-68), began the period of struggles between provinces. What interests us here is that this intestine war seems also to have been caused in part by a homosexual affair. When Ashikaga Yoshimasa (1435-90) took on the duties of shogun, real power was already in the hands of two powerful families, the Hosokawa and the Yamana. Yamana Sozen was the most influential: for his great deeds in the battles fought to punish Akamatsu Mitsusuke, he had received the province of Harima, one of the old fiefdoms of the Akamatsu. On the recommendation of Hosokawa Shigeyuki the shogun then took as a page a nephew of Akamatsu Mitsusuke. In love with this pretty page Norinao, he gave him permission to recover the province of Harima. Yamana Sozen was greatly angered, and considered this to be a plot by the Hosokawa. He attacked Norinao, who killed himself in a castle of Harima. The antagonism between the two clans of Yamana and Hosokawa afterwards became more and more violent, and finally the great Onin civil war broke out, and the two armies fought each other around the capital for nine years, and destroyed it utterly.

According to a document of the 16th century, the thirteenth shogun Yoshiteru also had a favourite called Matsui Sadonokami. Having reached the age of adulthood he entered the service of the Hosokawa, and his descendants are still to be found in this family. We may then suppose, on the basis of this short document, that the courageous page described in Frois's article succeeded Matsui Sadono-kami when the latter had left Yoshiteru.

Love among the samurai in the period of civil war
In a document about Hosokawa Takakuni (1484-1531), the grandson of Hosokawa Shigeyuki, we find the first example to highlight the characteristic feature of love as it existed among the samurai in the century of civil wars.

In the era of Yoshiharu the twelfth shogun, Hosokawa Takakuni was the most powerful nobleman. Yanagimoto Kenji, who had previously been his favourite, was his favoured vassal even after he had reached adulthood. Yanagimoto's elder brother, Kanishi Motomori, was the chief vassal of the Hosokawa clan. One day a cousin of Takakuni's, Hosokawa Iken, made a false accusation against Kanishi Motomori, with whom he was on bad terms. Deceived by these calumnies, the lord Takakuni decided to punish him with death. He thought nonetheless: 'If Kanishi dies, his brother Yanagimoto will not be able to remain in my service. I regret it! For once we swore to each other eternal love!' In the end he made a written oath in which he explained to his old favourite: 'I have punished your brother Kanishi. I had no other possibility, as he had conspired against me. As for you, I have toward you no disloyal feeling...' Then he sealed it, and put it in a letter-chest. After a few days, the lord called Kanishi to his palace to question him, but the deceitful Iken, pretending to misunderstand his lord's words, killed the accused with his sword. The lord was obliged to send the chest to Yanagimoto. He, having read the written oath, went hurriedly to present himself before the lord.

'My dear master,' he said, 'as my brother has been punished for the crime of conspiracy, I have no rancour against you, and I thank you earnestly for having been so good as to retain me in an employment as important as before.' With tears in his eyes he expressed his gratitude.

Many months later, Hatano Naomichi, the elder brother of Kanishi and Yanagimoto, left his province of Tamba and went to Kyoto so as to find out about this tragic affair. Discovering the truth, he returned quickly to his province, and with Yanagimoto raised an army to attack Iken.

Among the samurai of Hosokawa Takakuni, there was a young man called Takahata Jinkuro who was attached to Yanagimoto by ties of love. The evening of his secret departure, Yanagimoto paid him a visit, confessed his plans and asked if he would join with him. Having thought for a little while, Jinkuro answered his lover thus:

'I would like to go with you! Our friendship is well known, but I cannot break the oath of loyalty to my lord. Of course, I will keep your secret until you have raised your army. I wish you a good journey! I hope you will prepare as quickly as possible. But if we find ourselves in opposite camps, permit me to answer to you with an arrow.'

Thus it was that they parted from each other in tears, the one faithful to his master, the other loyal to his friendship.

This is told in the *Ashikaga kisei-ki*, or the 'Chronicle of the Ashikaga'.

2. Stories

(this section is an extract from Jun'ichi Iwata)

Loves of the beautiful Bansaku in the period of civil wars
In the century of the civil wars (16th c.), many young adolescents played an important role in historical events. Posterity would praise three of them in particular for their beauty of body and of spirit: Nagoshi Sanzaburu, page to Gamo Hidanokami, Asaka Shojiro, page to Kimura Isenokami, and Fuwa Bansaku, whose story we shall tell.

Among the many pages of the regent Hashiba Hidetsugu (1568-95), Bansaku was the prince's favourite. If Hidetsugu had been on good terms with his uncle Toyotomi Hideyoshi, the true dictator of the time, and if he had succeeded him in his political pre-eminence, Bansaku would have become a great lord of importance in Japanese history, as did Ishida Mitsunari,[2] Hideyoshi's own favourite. Unfortunately, being in disagreement with the dictator, Hidetsugu ended by being removed from his position, and he killed himself on Mount Koya. In consequence, the young man also died with his master in the flower of his youth, as when in full bloom the plum trees of Mount Koya are stripped bare by the cruel wind.

Hidetsugu as his successor and appointed him regent. As his second son Hideyori grew up, however, he began to want to replace Hidetsugu with his true son. Yodo-gimi, Hideyori's mother and his own favourite, was moreover continually asking that their child be named his successor. Ishida Mitsunari too, on bad terms with Hidetsugu, slandered him before the dictator. At this time Hideyoshi, putting into effect his plan for the conquest of Korea, had left the capital and was staying at Nagoya, a military port in Kyushu. The central government seemed then to be in the hands of his nephew, and this caused him some anxiety. When he heard of unreasonable acts by Hidetsugu, he naturally began to suspect his fidelity and ended by hating him. The slanders of Yodo-gimi, of Mitsunari and others also played a great part, as we have already noted.

Hidetsugu organised a hunting party only seventeen days after the death of the old *tenno*; he profaned the holy place of Mount Hiei by hunting over it, in the company of women even.[3] He killed a pregnant woman, tearing open her belly with an arrow. These were the 'unreasonable acts' which made his name live after him. We cannot take these accounts as true, for their source is the *Taiko-ki*, a

8. The affair of Sakuya, a *chigo* of the Myo'on-ji temple (p. 60).

9. Double suicide of a young monk and a servant (p. 60).

biography of Hideyoshi. It seems to me that most of these unbelievable events are of Mitsunari's invention. It seems likely, though, that Hidetsugu, giving himself much to pleasure like all those raised to high office, was fond of sumptuous banquets and even occasionally gave way to vice. In any event, having gained the hatred of his uncle Hideyoshi, he was sent to the monastery on Mount Koya, and killed himself there at the age of twenty-eight. His children and concubines were also killed and buried in a funerary mound at Kyoto, still known as 'Chikusho-zuka' or 'mound of brutes'.

When Hidetsugu committed suicide in the Seiganji temple on Mount Koya, Bansaku also killed himself, together with his lord's other favourites. According to the *Tensho-ki* or 'Chronicles of the Tensho era' (1572-86) by Ota Ushiichi, Hidetsugu himself helped three pages one after another to commit harakiri.[4] These were Yamamoto Tonoma, Yamada Sanjuro and Fuqa Bansaku. Having helped them, the lord died by cutting open his own belly. Bansaku was born in the province of Owari.

We still have some reports from the hand of Europeans on this tragic affair, although their accounts are sometimes suspect. According to the *History of Japan* (1669) drawn up by the Dutch Arnursus Montanus, the first to commit harakiri at the time of Hidetsugu's death was a page of 19 years. Hidetsugu, seeing this young man suffering in driving the sword into his belly, took him in his arms, cut off his head and put this on a plate on the table. He did the same thing for the other two pages.

Bansaku was without doubt the page the most loved by his master Hidetsugu. There remain to us few truthful documents relating to his life, and yet his beauty and his amorous adventures with men have been transmitted to us in stories which seem almost incredible. Three of them are told below.

In the stories about him, Bansaku, although in high favour with the regent, often sees into the hearts of those who fall in love with him and offers them, from compassion, the opportunity to see him in secret. Briefly, he seems to be an youth who knew how to commit adultery. He was well loved by his master, but nonetheless 'shared' his love with others, which certainly seems to us to be unfaithful and immoral. But from the point of view of those who suffered from an unhappy passion for their master's favourites, Bansaku was precisely an example of those 'youths of spirit' who understood the *shudo* perfectly. It is certain that lovers of young men greatly admired him as an ideal example, and it is likely then that in making an idol of Bansaku, they attributed to him many often incredible stories.

10. A page (*o-kosho*) unsheathing his sword. (From Ihara Saikaku's *Glorious Tales of Homosexuality* (1687), reproduced in Iwata's *Honcho danshoku ko.*)

11. 'The beautiful young Fuwa Bansaku', by the modern graphic artist Mitsuhiro Yoshida. (From *Shosetsu June*, no. 3, 1983, with the permission of Mr Yoshida.)

During his service as Hidetsugu's page, Bansaku's rare beauty was admired by all. Ogasawara Shinanonokami in particular adored him for a long time, but he could not reveal his passion because the regent took care to guard carefully the object of so many men's affection. Whenever he met the beautiful young man, all that Shinanonokami could do was to give him an adoring look, all unknown to their master. Bansaku soon noticed his feelings and, feeling sympathetic, replied to the look with his own. Shinanonokami, however, started more and more to show signs of being discontented with these wordless conversations, signs which Bansaku understood without difficulty. Seeing so much suffering in the eyes of Shinanonokami, he finally decided to see him personally. The lovers, however, were unable to find a spot where they might meet without being observed. Their suffering continued.

One day, the people of Kyoto would have seen in one of the avenues two palanquins which seemed wider than usual. When they came into the busy traffic of the avenue a strange thing happened; the two palanquins approached each other and seemed to get stuck together. Because of the congestion, however, the passers-by paid no attention to what the palanquins were doing. Soon they separated and went on their way. Towards the end of the day, the two palanquins became stuck together once more, and then separated again. Each then followed its own road as if nothing had happened. In fact, on that day Bansaku passed from one palanquin to another to see his lover Shinanonokami in secret – in the middle of streets crowded with passers-by, and nobody noticed! For Shinanonokami, it was a dream come true.

This is a little story, 'Inu tsurezure', from the second year of the Sho'o era (1653):

Each time the Regent passed by among the many numerous members of his escort, it was Bansaku more than anyone who drew attention. Pleased with, even proud of the rare beauty of his favourite, the Regent always wanted him at his side. As for Bansaku, he was deeply grateful for his master's favour, and did everything he could to serve him.

One day, he was accompanying his master as usual, when he noticed at Fukakusa a samurai standing at the side of the road. (Fukakusa is a village near Kyoto on the road to Fushimi, the site of Hidetsugu's castle.) Although Bansaku did not know him, when the young man passed by on horseback the unknown samurai greeted him politely. The unknown seemed still to be young and he looked the perfect samurai. Bansaku returned the greeting without paying attention. When he entered the castle of Fushimi with his master, he had already forgotten this little incident, for many behaved like this simply in order to express their admiration of his beauty.

Anyway, when he next went out on escort duty, he found the same samurai who greeted him in the same manner in the same place. It was impossible to pass by without seeing him. He replied to the samurai's greeting, and, for the first time, looked attentively at his face. The samurai looked back at him without a blink, and their eyes met for a second as the procession went on. The young man on the horse remained visible to the samurai for a few moments again, and then was hidden behind other people.

After these two little incidents, which no one else had noticed, Bansaku spent his time wondering what was in the heart of the unknown samurai. He was always with his lord, and enjoyed his favour, but it was impossible not to dream about this stranger.

'Seemingly, this gentleman is not an inhabitant of the capital. He must come from some province. But why should he wait many times for me at the side of the road and greet me so politely? It is true that I can guess what is in his heart, especially from his eyes the moment that he looked at me. But he too must surely be in the service of some lord. How is it that he can wait for me at Fukakusa each time I go towards Kyoto? Or were the two meetings a mere chance? Let's see the next day I do escort duty!'

Abandoning himself to his imagination, Bansaku waited for the next time he should go to Kyoto. In his dreams, the samurai had already become a man worthy of confidence.

The day came when the Regent eventually went to Kyoto. Bansaku followed him as usual. When the procession approached the village of Fukakusa he set his horse to a walk and looked about him with beating heart. To his surprise, he found the samurai at the side of the road once more. Bansaku greeted the samurai first, and the other replied hurriedly to this greeting, looking fixedly at the young man on the horse. Bansaku saw that he had tears in his eyes, and once more made a slight bow. As the procession passed, they grew further and further away from each other.

Each time he was on duty in the procession, the same thing happened to him. Now Bansaku knew very well what was in the heart of the strange samurai. But why was he always around Fukakusa? Where did he live? To answer these questions, one day when they were in procession he had his servant follow the unknown secretly and find out his dwelling.

According to the servant when he returned in the evening, the samurai in question lived alone in the village of Fukakusa. He had not wished to divulge his identity, but when the servant told him he was sent by Bansaku, he was moved to tears and told him his sad story.

12. Complementarity of yin and yang (p. 65).

13. The servant Kochibei and wishes come true (p. 66).

14. The Tsuneuemon
affair, brought about by
jealousy (p. 69).

He had earlier been in the service of a great lord of Kyushu. One day, when he came to the capital on business, he met by chance with the Regent's procession and there found a very beautiful young man with whom he immediately fell in love. From then onward, the image of Bansaku had never left him. If it was impossible to gratify his desire, he wished at least to look upon the youth's fair face so as to calm his passion. Finally he asked his master for permission to leave, and had begun a solitary life in the village of Fukakusa. In all his sad life his only joy was to watch the beautiful young man each time the Regent's procession went by. Hearing this astounding story, Bansaku's heart grew tender. It was impossible to ignore the passion of this young samurai, so sincere, even if it might seem ungrateful to his lord.

'This gentleman,' he thought, 'has abandoned everything for love of me. And yet he is not hopeful, but only sadly resigned. Ready to live with this resignation, he has really given up everything. His only pleasure is to look at me in secret when the procession passes. But how is it possible? How has he lived until today, supported by no more than so modest a hope?' At first he thought to respond to the love of the samurai only from duty. But the more he thought about what attitude to adopt, the happier he felt at being loved by a man having such a heart of gold. 'His good appearance, his burning eyes, he is a true samurai!' In his imagination, Bansaku was already at the house in Fukakusa where at that very moment the errant samurai doubtless mourned his unhappy love.

A few days later, a messenger of Bansaku's came to the samurai in secret. He gave him a long letter, and went away immediately. The samurai read it and reread it many times. His hot tears flowed ceaselessly, and he found, eventually, that without his noticing it, the letter paper, perfumed with the smoke of incense, had become completely wet.

Some days later, the Regent Hidetsugu decided upon a hunt at Hirano. Bansaku accompanied him as usual. He dressed himself, however, with more magnificence than usual. His face was radiant the whole day through, and there was nobody who did not praise the young man's grace. When the sun set and the company were about to return to the castle, the face of Bansaku, who had all the time been at the side of the regent, suddenly clouded, and he complained of a pain in the belly. The handsome favourite's sudden illness upset the Regent and his gentlemen-in-waiting. They hurried to obtain a room at the temple of Ishiyama-dera near Hirano, and they left the patient there with a doctor and some servants.

Happily, Bansaku got better quickly, thanks to the doctor's treatment perhaps. Then he organised a small feast to celebrate his recovery. Night fell on Ishiyama-dera, and everyone fell down drunk. But Bansaku was not drunk. He didn't even seem to have been ill only a little while before. Late at night, he left the room on tiptoe without making a sound. He passed the wall of the temple, and then walked in the dark towards the bridge of Seta. When he reached the bridge, there was a shadow leaning on the parapet. Bansaku stopped, and called out, shyly but eagerly.

It was the samurai from Fukakusa, whose only pleasure had been secretly to look on Bansaku's face. He approached his beloved, taking off the cloak that he had worn to hide himself. They had not spoken yet, but they understood each other perfectly. The samurai was enveloped in the perfume of the precious incense which the young man used.

But the Regent, back at his castle already, was so worried about Bansaku that he decided to send Ueda Mondonosho to see how he was. The faithful Mondonosho, having listened respectfully to his master's command, left on horseback, as quickly as he could. When he reached the bridge of Seta he smelt a distinctive perfume.

'That is not a common perfume. It is my master's favourite incense!' said Mondonosho to himself. 'Now I need not go all the way to the temple of Ishiyama-dera, for I know very well who usually uses this incense when he's with my lord.'

So, leaving his grooms behind, he went alone onto the bridge and cried out in a loud voice to the two shadows hardly visible in the black night:

'Bansaku? It is I, Ueda Mondonosho, sent by our master. I think I know why you are there; but I will report to our master in such a way that all will be well for you.' And he turned and left, quickly.

Bansaku, hearing these words in the dark, was moved to tears by Mondo-nosho's goodwill. Holding his lover in his arms, he said to him:

'We are saved! But it is impossible always to count on such good luck or such goodwill. If my lord should one day learn our secret...'

The samurai, who understood his beloved's perplexity, lowered his head and said not a word. Bansaku continued:

'My love for you will never alter, but it seems almost impossible to see you secretly again. I beg you, take my linen, for a consolation, as a memorial of our love.'

The youth took off his *kosode* (a white undergarment worn beneath the *furi-sode*), and gave it to his lover. As the white linen gave off an exquisite perfume, the samurai dissolved in tears.

Bansaku returned to the temple of Ishiyama-dera before daybreak. There indeed was a transient moment of delight, whose only souvenir, for the samurai, was the scented *kosode*. Because Ueda Mondonosho never spoke of it, their secret remained their own, and lord Hidetsugu loved his dearest Bansaku as much as ever.

After leaving his beloved, the samurai of Fukakusa killed himself at dawn, opening up his belly and throwing himself into Lake Biwa. He no longer had any reason to live, because he had realised his heart's desire. His body floated for a little time and finally came to ground at Shiga. The people there found that the dead man was wearing a white linen undergarment with long sleeves, like that worn by a page to a great lord. They were impressed by the exquisite perfume given off by this *kosode*. Bansaku, hearing this news, secretly obtained the body and buried him with care in a temple cemetery at Shiga.

In the summer of the fourth year of the Bunroku era (1595), when the lord Hidetsugu was about to die, he asked those of his subjects who were to die with him to tell him freely what they were thinking. No one dared speak, except Bansaku. He told the story of the samurai, weeping as he spoke.

He sincerely asked forgiveness for his infidelity towards his master. His lord was also brought to tears by the moving passion of the poor samurai.

The final story is told in the fifth volume of the *Shin Chomon shu*, published in the Kan'ei era (1624-29):

About the time of the Bunroku era (1592-96), a monk called Master Imyo lived at the temple Horin-ji at Saga, the great western suburb of Kyoto.

One winter's day he left for Kyoto, accompanied by a servant, and when he got to Katahira-no-tsuji, snow began to fall. When they passed close to Uzumasa, the countryside was already completely covered in snow. Walking with difficulty, they arrived at the forest of Kitano, near the city of Kyoto.

Just then, the master saw a young man coming towards them, with his umbrella up. He seemed to be walking quickly, but with some difficulty. They met by a large pine tree, and at that moment the master was fascinated by an exquisite perfume.

'Who is this elegant young man,' he wondered, looking directly at him.

Ah! Behind the umbrella was a young man of an incomparable beauty, a beauty which astounded him and kept him rooted to the spot! This young man was Bansaku. In the morning, the Regent Hidetsugu had left to go to see the sight of the temple of the Golden Pavilion in the snow. But on the way it occurred to him that he might play the flute while he was there. It was for this that Bansaku, the Regent's favourite lover, had returned immediately to the Jurakudai palace at

Kyoto and was now with his master's flute in hand, quickly making his way towards the temple, despite the snow.

The young man passed by the monk with indifference, but as soon as he had done so, he tripped and fell over a pine root, and his pretty sandals were flung some distance away from him. The master hurried to help him to his feet. He carefully brushed the snow from the young man's robe. Finding that one of the straps of the sandals was broken, he set himself to replace it with a cord that he had with him. (The ancient Japanese used to carry a spare cord with them when travelling, because the straps of their sandals were a weak point.)

A moment later, when the repair was finished, Bansaku received with respect the repaired sandal to which the monk had devoted all his heart. He asked the monk for his name and address. After having introduced himself, the beautiful young man left the place with the promise that they would meet again one day.

From that day on, the image of the youth never left the monk. Happily for the master, he discovered that one of Bansaku's servants was the brother of a craftsman who lived before the temple of Horin-ji. 'Here is providential aid!' cried the master. Without delay, he secretly sent to Bansaku, through this brother, a letter into which he had poured all his heart.

He waited impatiently for the youth's reply. Here is the text of the letter which he finally received, and which he read with beating heart:

> How could I forget your kindness, which saved me from great difficulty? I am deeply indebted to you. As to what you have written to me, I am a little frightened, and I am troubled in conscience, for my master loves me greatly. But despite this, your letter has very much moved me. Indeed, since that snowy day, your image has not left me.
>
> It is, however, very difficult, as you know, to arrange a meeting. The first day of the Ox, in the month of Kisaragi (February), seems to me to be the only one possible, for on that day all the villagers visit the Shinto chapel of Uga no Mitama in the park of the castle of Fushimi. Turn to the left above the old pine beside the chapel, then go along the path to the stable, behind which you will find a seal affixed to a tree. Wait for me there, I beg you.
>
> It is a very dangerous adventure. Do not forget that no one can save us from death if, by chance, my lord should learn of our secret. And I beg of you, after this, do not ask for another meeting...

The day arrived at last for which Master Imyo had waited with such patience. Among the visitors to the chapel, he succeeded in entering the castle grounds. Then he looked for the place arranged, where he saw his beloved Bansaku. Tears came to his eyes. Bansaku took him silently by the hand and led him behind the stable. Both of them, fearing to be discovered, stayed silent till the end.

They parted at nightfall with interminable farewells. Towards midnight, the master arrived back at his temple, in a state of great excitement.

From that day, the master did not any longer try to see Bansaku. He restrained his passion for the young man. He had perfectly understood what Bansaku had written at the end of his letter. When he learnt the news of the young man's death on Mount Koya, he was plunged into grief. But he recovered himself quickly, and spent his life praying to the Buddha, so they say, for the peace of his old beloved.

This anecdote is to be found in the *Harusame monogatari* of Takai Ranzan, which appeared in the first year of the Kan'ei era (1624).

Complementarity of Yin and Yang

A Confucian of the Edo period, Ota Kinjo (1765-1825), wrote: 'The sexual desire of men ascends, while that of women descends.' According to his Essays, when a man gives free rein to his desire, he wants naturally to form a liaison with his superior, as fire flames upward. This is because man is *yo* (the positive, active, luminous and celestial principle, yang). When woman is free, on the other hand, she wishes to form a liaison with her inferior, for she is *in* (the negative, passive, dark and terrestrial principle, yin). She is as water which flows downward.

Men wish to rape their mistress, while women wish to commit adultery with their servant and with the lower classes. Mr Ota cites many historical characters to illustrate this idea. He carries his argument to its conclusions, saying that even if there are contrary examples, they are due to financial or other impure motives.

I do not know if he invented this strange idea himself, but it interests me greatly. I too can find illustrations of the 'descending sexual desire' of women, in the relations between Izumi Shikibu and a peasant, known through a story in the *Kokon chomon shu*, and, as a recent example, the affair between countess Kamako and her indentured driver.

This idea can also be applied, it seems to me, to amorous intrigue between men!

Men who are in easy circumstances have a gentle character and an inclination to femininity, tending to like young men of a lower class than they, while those of lower condition often admire the feminine beauty of boys in high society.

On the other hand, there can be contrary cases. Love is not a matter easy to analyse from the outside. And to the extent that one has to think about the problems of dignity and of *giri* (duty) in society, the homosexual liaison is even more difficult to explain. But to illustrate this idea, I will give various examples from literary and historical works of the past.

The servant Koichibei and wishes come true

In a play entitled 'Double Suicide in the Middle of the Night', written in the sixth year of Kyoho (1721), Chikamatsu Monzaemon deals with the love-suicide of two lovers, O-chiyo and Hanbei. The first act, however, has no relation to what is to follow later; it consists of an independent episode which deals ingeniously with the homosexual affairs of Hanbei's half-brother Koshichiro. Here is an outline:

A beautiful young man called Yamawaki Koshichiro was the page of an old samurai Sakabe Gozaemon, who lived in the town of Hamamatsu in the province of Totoumi. His half-brother Hanbei, who was now a merchant despite being the son of a samurai, was staying at Hamamatsu for the seventeenth anniversary memorial service for their father.

Koshichiro's beauty had for some time been attracting men to the house of Mr Sakabe. There were notably Kaneda Jinzo, Oka Gun'uemon and Ohashi Ippei, junior officers to Mr Sakabe, who were strongly attached to the young man and had sent him many love-letters; but they had not yet succeeded in divining his true feelings.

One day, the three samurai came to Hanbei and started a discussion in which each hoped to overcome his rivals in love. Hanbei, however, was reluctant to confirm the hopes of any one of them, as if he did not know what was in his brother's heart. At that moment, Koshichiro himself appeared. Seventeen years old, at the height of his beauty as a *chigo*, with his jet-black hair falling over his forehead, he cast a seductive look at each of the three samurai, and put down a heap of letters in front of his brother, saying:

'Despite the shame I have before my brother, I can no longer hide these things. I am very grateful for the love you have offered me, who am without importance. It will leave happy memories of the days when I dressed in the *furi-sode* (see Ill. 3). There are, however, too many letters from too many gentlemen; I accepted them because it would have been unkind to send them back, but I have not opened one. I give them back to you unopened, and I beg you sirs, to give me up!'

It seemed to Hanbei, on the other hand, that his younger brother was hiding his real intentions behind these words. Hanbei said:

66

'I, who am now a merchant, but in my heart a true samurai, will give my brother Koshichiro to the one who really loves him. I will myself choose his lover. Koshichiro! go and dress yourself in white!' Guessing his brother's intention, the young man went straightaway to his room. Hanbei, reading each of the signatures on so many love-letters, found many signed 'Koichibei'. 'Who is this Koichibei?' he asked, for there was none of that name among the three samurai.

'This Koichibei is a servant in the house,' replied the three samurai, laughing in a mocking fashion. 'How ridiculous that such a vulgar creature should pay court to our young man!'

'Not at all!' interrupted Hanbei, 'I am not of your opinion. In this Way there is no question of difference of rank. I will call Koichibei and consider him as one of the candidates for love.' A little later, Koshichiro appeared in the costume of harakiri, as if prepared for death, that is to say in a white *kosode* and a *kamishimo* (the formal dress of a samurai, pale yellow on the outside) (see Ill. 30). Hanbei put two swords in front of the young man, their blades bare, and said:

'Four claimants for just one youth! Even if I gave him to one gentleman, the three others would remain resentful. I am the more nervous in that I live far from here in a distant province. As these are distinguished samurai who appeal to me, a simple merchant, there is no way of escape. It is because of this I have had him dress in white and prepare for death. Gentlemen! if you love my dear Koshichiro so much, you may cherish him as well in another world. Die with him here, with this sword. You may be lover and *wakashu* in the beyond, where nobody will trouble you. I will give my dear little brother to any one among you who will swear eternal love! Why do you not do it?' His expression, suddenly become threatening, terrified the samurai. They couldn't say a word, being overcome by fear.

The servant Koichibei was only a provincial of low birth, but he had admired Koshichiro for a long time, and had written to him so many times because he could not give up his desperate love, despite their difference of rank. Suddenly finding himself called for, he went hurriedly and found, beyond all his expectations, that Hanbei was counting him among the candidates. On hearing Hanbei's words he was overcome by joy. He snatched up one of the swords in front of the young man and was on the point of plunging it into his belly. Koshichiro took the other sword and was going to kill himself as well. Hanbei rushed between the two and restrained them with difficulty, holding them by the arm.

'Sir!' cried Koichibei, 'if I may not die here I shall have no way of showing my eternal love for my adorable *wakashu*. Let me die now!'

His decided attitude on the threshold of death greatly impressed Hanbei, who himself cried out:

'Verily, you are a true man. You are the only one to love Koshichiro sincerely. Now that it is clear that my dear Koshichiro has only one true lover, why should I command him to die? I beg you, dear Koichibei, to look after my brother as his lover.'

'Oh...yes!'

He cried tears of joy, and leapt into the arms of the young man dressed in white, who held against his own breast this Koichibei dressed in his worker's clothes, a dark blue *happi*. In the aloe-wood perfume of the white *kosode*, and the smell of the blue dye of the *happi*, the lovers sobbed together.

And so it is that the Koichibei of the 'Double Suicide in the Middle of the Night' triumphs over his rivals in love. His success may be attributed to the fact that Koshichiro had understood the difference between his absolute love and the frivolous love of the three samurai.

In *kabuki* works, after the second third of the Edo period, one sometimes finds an affair of the heart between a princess and a servant, generally with the princess falling in love with a servant who is unfeeling. As regards the 'Double Suicide...', because the page Koshichiro says so little, we cannot tell whose passion is the stronger. But considering the speeches and attitudes of the other characters, it would seem that it is first of all Koshichiro who falls in love. And it even seems that the two brothers may have planned together beforehand.

Testing the sincerity of rivals in love by placing two swords with bare blades before the youth reminds me of certain homosexual customs of a military character from the province of Satsuma. Here is an example:

In the autumn of the tenth year of the Kan'ei era (1637), the marquis of Satsuma left for battle at the head of eight thousand soldiers, ordered to repress the Shimabara revolt in the province of Hisen; it was necessary to reinforce the frontier guard between Satsuma and Hisen.

Yamada Matsunosuke, son of the lord of the town of Demizu, near the frontier, was the chief of the frontier guards. Matsunosuke was a boy of fifteen years of age, of great intelligence and unequalled beauty. When he left on his horse, dressed as a general in great magnificence, he looked like one of the Taira princes (the Taira were the first military clan that came to power in the 12th century), and all the people of Demizu came to the gate of the castle to admire him and to walk alongside. The young samurai, who had been in love with Matsunosuke for a long time, were so impressed by his fine and splendid military dress that they swore, inwardly, that they would fight and die on the field of honour before the eyes of their handsome general.

The following year, when the revolt had been defeated, the lord returned from Hisen and gave a banquet at the castle to celebrate the victory. The young samurai were impressed by their lord's having his son Matsunosuke pour sake for each of them, a great honour for a samurai.

It was a fine precedent; the samurai of Demizu, and later those of Satsuma would always choose a young adolescent as captain when they went on active duty, even in time of peace. And when they organised a banquet, they would ask him to pour sake for them, honouring him as a samurai.

This youth chosen and appointed captain was called *torimochi chigo*, (*torimochi* meaning 'appointed'). Here is one of the interesting amusements of the samurai of Satsuma, amongst whom homosexuality was so popular. The first to be served by the *torimochi chigo* at a banquet was considered to be very lucky, and everyone fell upon him all at once and snatched a few of his hairs, so as to 'share in his luck'.

The Tsuneuemon affair, brought about by jealousy

Here is a true story of the Kyoho era (1716-35), set down in the *History of the Manners of Kyoho*:

Kano Tsuneuemon, in the service of Akimoto Iganokami, had for a very long time been intimate with Inaba Sasuke, a servant of Manabe Wakasanokami. Not only did they both belong to the *ashigaru*, the lowest class of the samurai, but they were united in the *shudo*.

Tsuneuemon loved Sasuke without hiding it, although the latter was easily ten years younger than he. For his part, Sasuke also trusted Tsuneuemon as if he were his own brother. Time passed, and in the tenth year of the Kyoho era, Tsuneuemon was thirty years old and Sasuka twenty. It seemed now to Tsuneuemon that his beloved did not see him as often as he used to, which sometimes worried him.

It is understandable that time separates friends, especially in a case such as this where each was in the service of a different master.

In the early years, they used to see each other by meeting at the place of work of the one who was last to finish. Their greatest pleasure was to go out together when work was over. As they got to know their fellow-workers, however, it is probable that they occasionally directed their affections towards others.

Tsuneuemon, old enough and mature in his judgment, did not take change easily. Sasuke, on the other hand, was still young. He must have been very beautiful too, to judge by the strength of Tsuneuemon's attachment.

Tsuneuemon often thought about the recent cooling-off of their relationship. He feared that his beloved's feelings might change, despite the fact that he still loved him greatly. Perhaps he sometimes confessed his anxiety and asked for confirmation of their *shudo* union. The young man must then have been meekness itself.

Yet this very meekness provoked anxiety in Tsuneuemon. Sasuke, guessing what lay behind Tsuneuemon's dark expression, must have become fearful of him, which would have caused the relationship to deteriorate even further. As Tsuneuemon's concern became ever stronger, the young man began to want to be rid of his lover.

It is probable too that Sasuke, like many beautiful young men, was deep inside a little feminine and capricious.

In this tense situation, strange news spread through the household of Manabe Wakasanokami and came to the ears of Tsuneuemon. Sasuke had entered into a *shudo* union with a new lover while hiding it from Tsuneuemon.

On January 25th of the tenth year of the Kyoho era, Tsuneuemon took his treacherous beloved to the house of Saburobei Genroku, Sasuke's guardian. We cannot know what was then his intention. As for Sasuke, did he still pretend friendship, as he followed Tsuneuemon? Did Tsuneuemon reproach him for his infidelity and beg him to return to his old love? What did Sasuke say in reply? In the short note in the *History of the Customs of Kyoho* we find none of these details.

In any case, the consequence of these events was that in Genroku's house, where his wife was alone, Tsuneuemon killed the young man with a blow of his sword and then cut open his own belly. When Genroku returned, he saw a bloody scene in his house: Tsuneuemon had not succeeded in killing himself with the first stroke, and was writhing in pain at the side of his dead beloved. Genroku quickly reported the affair to the police. It seems that Tsuneuemon died, but this is not reported in the note.

The affair of Sakuya, a *chigo* of the Myo'on-ji temple

In the Kanbun era (1661-63), there was a young man named Sajiuemon, the son of a wholesaler in the town of Okayama. Having worked elsewhere for some years, he returned to the house of his father, where he lived a life of idleness. To escape boredom he went every day to the temple of Myofuku-ji where he played ball. He noticed that a young and very beautiful youth named Sakuya used to often come and watch him play; he was the favourite of the head of the Myo'on-ji temple which stood not far away. Falling in love with him, Sajiuemon made every effort to win the young man's heart, and eventually succeeded. From then on, they loved each other greatly, without concern for what others should think.

One evening, the tenth of June, having finished his game, Sajiuemon suddenly addressed himself to his friend Mogami Genpachi, who happened to be at Myofuku-ji: 'Call Sakuya from Myo'on-ji for me, if you would. I absolutely must see him, for I am going to kill him with my knife!' Genpachi, astonished, asked him why.

'Recently, I have called for him two or three times, but he has never come. And so, tonight, I have decided to kill him.' He was in such a fury that Genpachi, seeing that there was no way to change his mind, was obliged to go away. Sajiuemon, left alone at Myofuku-ji, had himself to call for Sakuya, but in vain. Eventually he went in to Myo'on-ji, and brought Sakuya out.

As they walked together in the night, the man reproached the boy for his recent coolness. Hearing him make only evasive replies, he believed that his beloved had already decided to leave him and so declared to the boy his intention to kill him.

Sakuya looked sadly at his lover and replied: 'If you wish to kill me, I can only submit. But I beg of you, let me have a little time to see my old mother once again!'

Agreeing to the boy's wishes, Sajiuemon took him to the house of his mother, who lived in the village of Nakajima. She was surprised at their unexpected visit, and wondered what had happened to her son. Sakuya made up a plausible excuse and left soon afterwards, perhaps forever.

Then they wandered through the night. Sakuya, ready for death, urged his lover to kill him as soon as possible. But Sajiuemon, having pronounced the sentence in anger, could not bring himself to carry out his initial plan, for he still loved the boy deeply.

'My darling Sakuya, forgive me! I didn't really intend to kill you. I said that, it's true, but it was only to test the sincerity of your heart. Now, do not die! Let us go together to the house of Iba Gonzaemon, administrator of the village of Matsuo. He is a trustworthy man. Forgive me for what I did, I beg of you!'

The relationship between Iba Gonzaemon and Sajiuemon was not clear. They saw the administrator of Matsuo, who allowed them to stay with him. There they remained until the thirteenth.

While this had been going on, Mogami Genpachi had returned home, having left his friend alone at Myofuku-ji, and was beginning to get worried. That evening, he visited Sajiuemon's father, and saw that his friend had not yet returned home. The next day he went twice to visit his friend, but without success. Saburobei, Sajiuemon's father, finally began to suspect these frequent visits by his son's friend, and asked him whether his son had suffered some accident. It was in this way that the old merchant learnt for the first time of the relations between his son and the *chigo* from Myo'on-ji. Greatly astonished, he begged Genpachi to look for Sajiuemon.

That evening Genpachi wrote to Iba Gonzaemon, because according to Saburobei, that was where his son would probably be. The administrator of Matsuo replied that Sajiuemon was not at his house, but asked him to come and see him because he too was worried about Sajiuemon.

On the twelfth, Genpachi visited the administrator and was able to see his friend and Sakuya. The whole night, he did what he could to persuade him to come home, but all in vain. The following day, having said all that he could, Genpachi returned to the house of Saburobei and told him all that had happened.

On the morning of the fourteenth, the old merchant and his wife, greatly grieving, went to see Gonzaemon to ask him to give them back their son. They learnt that the two lovers had wanted to go away, and that the administrator had given them some money for the journey and had accompanied them as far as the next village.

The old couple went home in despair. Eight days later, a search having been made, the lovers were arrested at Osaka, a fair distance from Okayama. They were sent straight back to their province, and were brought to trial on July 1st, before the lord of Okayama. He particularly wanted to know why Sajiuemon and Sakuya had neither of them wished to return to their homes, despite the advice of Genpachi and of Gonzaemon.

Being questioned, Sakuya replied:

'My Lord, it was I that wished it! Sajiuemon had told me to go quickly back to my mother. But he said too that he would kill himself by harakiri after taking me back. So I refused to go, and I told him that I would kill myself by biting off my tongue if I was forced to go home. I cannot survive alone, for I have already betrayed my master at Myo'on-ji. Mr Iba Gonzaemon, hearing of my resolution, said, "Well, this is a sincere and courageous boy. If we force him, he will kill himself by biting off his tongue, I am sure of it. Don't you think so, Sajiuemon?" '

Sajiuemon, Genpachi and Gonzaemon all confirmed these words, showing on their faces their admiration for the young man.

The Court ordered the administrator Iba to kill himself by harakiri, and sentenced Sajiuemon to be beheaded. Sakuya was acquitted, but we do not know what became of him afterwards.

This fairly extensive note is found in the *Kibi onko hiroku*, or 'Secret Stories of the Kibi Country, Wherein to Regret Times Past', compiled by Osawa Koresada, a vassal of the lord of Okayama, in the Kansei era (1789-1801).

Double suicide of a young monk and a servant

Here is another true story, recorded in the second volume of 'A Word for Every Story' by Ota Atushi:

In July of the first year of the Tenmei era (1781), in the forest of Suginawate in the province of Suruga, two lovers killed themselves for love: a man of more than thirty years of age, and a young monk of seventeen to eighteen.

The origin of this tragedy was that the man, a servant of the Hotai-ji temple, had fallen in love with a young monk from another temple at the foot of Mount Fuji. The latter was the favourite of the head of the temple. Had he loved this poor servant from another temple more than he loved his master? Having heard of their love, had the head of the temple placed obstacles in their way? Had they both lost any hope of obtaining in this world what they most desired? Or did this poor menial, overcome by passionate love, bring his beloved to death by force? We cannot know. The author tells us only that the man, having killed the young monk, did not succeed in killing himself immediately. When he was discovered by villagers, he was still clinging to the dead body. It seems that this was much talked about as an extraordinary event, even at that time, when homosexual affairs and lovers' double suicides were not indeed uncommon.

(end of extract from Juni'chi Iwata)

IV. The Love of Boys in the Theatre

1. The development of the theatre from no to kabuki

The love of *chigo* overflows the monastery and reaches the court
From the 12th century, the last quarter of the Heian era, the love of the *chigo* passed beyond monastery walls and became fashionable at Court. The ex-emperor and despot Shirakawa-In (1053-1129), who ruled Japan for 43 years after leaving the throne, was particularly fond of homosexual pleasure. At this time (1072-1156) there was a curious custom whereby the emperor appointed his son as his successor and then abdicated so as to take hold of the real power. The abdicated emperor was called the *In*, and this original arrangement the *In-sei*, that is to say an 'abdicated administration'. This was a scheme by the emperors to escape the influence of the 'family of regents', the aristocratic clan of the Fujiwara. It was during this era, it is said, that the custom began of having favourites at the palace. The next ex-emperor, Toba-no-In (1103-56), was also an admirer of beautiful boys. A poet and lover of music, he was particularly fond of *chigo* dancing. From his era onward, the habit of powdering oneself, painting false eyebrows, using perfume and dressing very elegantly seems to have become popular among the men of high society. Toba-no-In, it is said, wished his favourites to powder themselves, to paint on false eyelashes, perfume themselves and dress as elegantly as young girls. Some even say that the fashion for make-up and beautiful clothes was then introduced into the monasteries and made the monks' own favourites even more delightful.

This homosexual taste was soon welcomed by the warrior class, a growing force at the time. In fact the princes of the Taira, the first military clan to come to power (1159), imitated the fashion of the nobles and dressed with a gaudy elegance like the women of the court.

During the Kamakura era (1184-1333), it seems that the samurai were less attracted towards these customs, perhaps because their centre of activity, the *bakufu* or 'shogunate' established by Minamoto no Yoritomo, was at Kamakura, very far from Kyoto. The situation changed, however, as soon as the Ashikaga established the new shogunate in the middle of Kyoto, the centre of aristocratic tradition. As the shoguns and great lords willingly adopted the graceful customs of the court of the Tenno, that of having young favourites was also introduced into their palaces. Ashikaga Yoshimitsu, the third shogun, is especially remembered as a great patron of the arts (today especially remembered as the builder of the Golden Pavilion[1]) and was also known in his own time for his fondness for homosexuality. It is against this background that Zeami, the great actor, author and theoretician of *no* drama, made his brilliant appearance.

Shogun Yoshimitsu and the young actor Fujiwaka

In 1374, Yoshimitsu attended a *sarugaku* performance at the Shinto temple of Imagumano. The *sarugaku*, or 'dance of the monkeys', was then one of the popular entertainments. The companies, under the patronage of certain great temples, gave performances, often of an edifying character, during the religious festivals, rather like the mystery plays of the European Middle Ages. This theatre, hitherto regarded as vulgar, was highly regarded by the shogun. He was particularly taken by the playing of Kan'ami (1333-84) and by the beauty of his son Fujiwaka, who was eleven years old. He very soon brought them to his Court. From then on, the *sarugaku*, later called *sarugaku no no*, or simply *no*, developed under the protection of the shoguns. Kan'ami died ten years later. His successor Fujiwaka, now called Zeami, revealed himself as an incomparable genius. During his long life of eighty years, he wrote words and music for forty plays, and left twenty-one books of theory, always trying to realise the *yugen*,[2] the aesthetic ideal of the *no* theatre. *No* would have remained, like the 'dance of the monkeys', merely an entertainment for the lower classes if it had not been for Yoshimitsu's protection of Zeami. The great shogun favoured the young actor not only for his prodigious talent but also for his beauty.

Was Fujiwaka really a beautiful boy? There is evidence of it in a noble's letter. When Fujiwaka was thirteen years old, Ichijo Sanekane, a poet and 'arbiter elegantiae' of the period, wrote to his friend: 'If Fujiwaka is free, by any chance, I beg you to bring him to my house once again. When I saw him, I was in the clouds all day long... What most captivated me were his face and his graceful manners, both sweet and masculine at the same time. I had never thought there could be such a perfect young boy in all the world... My lord the shogun is certainly right to hold him in affection.'

In what way was this boy 'held in affection' by the shogun? We may read a passage describing it in the diary of a minister of the period. Fujiwaka was sixteen, and the minister deplored the fact that the shogun went to see a festival performance in the young man's company.

'My lord the shogun, since some years, holds in affection a young performer of *sarugakuru*, and sometimes sits down to table with him. The *sarugaku* was originally a most lowly occupation. Yet... those who offer many presents to this young man please my lord. And so many great lords willingly give him costly gifts. They spend millions.'

Apart from Fujiwaka, Yoshimitsu had many other favourites, such as Ongamaru, Keigamaru, Kijumaru and Kikuwakamaru. There is no doubt that the relation between the shogun and the young actor was of a sexual nature, despite the doubts of modern historians. Our great Zeami was the favourite of a shogun in his youth; which is not in the least a stain on the history of *no*, whatever modern historians might think. In modern *no*, everything happens in an austere and hidden manner; at its origin, however, it was a voluptuous and sometimes even erotic spectacle in which young actors vied with each other not only in skill but also in beauty.

Between homosexuality and the *no* of the 14th century there exists an indissoluble link. This is equally the case for the *kabuki* of the 17th, as we shall see later.

The impossibility of appreciating certain *no* plays without understanding the homosexual tradition

One cannot fully appreciate certain plays without an understanding of the homosexual tradition of the Middle Ages.[3] In the play Kaguetsu, for example (Ill. 15), a monk travels through Kyoto, and in front of the temple of Kiyomizu-dera he sees the dance of a *kasshiki*, that is to say a young man who is both juggler and prostitute. The monk, a former samurai, became a monk after the disappearance of his only child, and is now on a pilgrimage. He soon finds out, to his great surprise, that this pretty *kasshiki*, called Kaguetsu, is his own son. Kidnapped at the age of nine by some *tengu*, legendary creatures of the mountains, ridiculously dressed with long noses and wings (Ill. 16), the boy wandered with them from mountain to mountain. While dancing he tells the whole of his incredible tale, and at the end, leaves on pilgrimage in the company of his father. What then is the meaning of this absurd kidnapping by the *tengu*? The *tengu* are really *yamabushi*, a kind of hermit that wanders through the mountains. The truth is, then, that the poor boy was captured by licentious *yamabushi*. He was probably passed from one to another as a sex object, and then became this juggler who occasionally resorted to prostitution.

16. Two costumes from *no* theatre: of a 'god incarnate in the form of an angelic boy', and of a *tengu*. (From *Nihon koten bungaku taikei*, vol. 41, Iwanami Shoten, 1963. By permission of the author, Mario Yokomichi.)

15. A scene from *Kagetsu*. The *kasshiki* Kagetsu is dancing. Performed by
the Kanze association of *no* actors, Kyoto.

Today, many people enjoy plays such as Kaguetsu, either in the text or in performance, without recognising their homosexual connotation. As a result, their eroticism and truly tragic quality are today lost on them all; *no* often seems boring and inaccessible to the spectators, to young people especially. The truth is that we moderns, having lost the cultural tradition of homosexuality, have equally lost the sensibility essential to the appreciation of *no*.

Travelling players introduce homosexuality to the provincial population

The development of *no* went hand in hand with the popularisation of the cultural tradition of homosexuality. Throughout the 15th and 16th centuries, this spread steadily outward, from the upper classes to the people, from the capital to the provinces.

One of the principal causes of this dissemination is the extension of the activity of the *sarugaku no no* companies from the capital to the provinces. At that time there were six great *no* fraternities in the capital, amongst which was the Kanze school founded by Kan'ami and Zeami. They were all under the protection of important temples, sometimes of the shogun, and they survive today in the names of the six schools of *no*. Most of the numerous minor companies born of the vogue for *no* had to tour from province to province. To attract their clients, they relied on the sexual attractions of their young men, rather than on their art. They often went so far even as to prostitute their younger members in order to survive. Influenced by these companies of travelling players, small companies arose in the provinces themselves, which also offered as their chief feature the erotic attractions of their handsome young men. The authors of a 15th-century book of travels record the universal fashion for homosexuality in the provinces, and the existence of boys who were both performers and prostitutes.

Love of the *chigo* and love of the *wakashu*

The best documentary help we have for understanding what homosexuality was to the people of the provinces is a *kyogen* piece (a little farce played as an interlude between *no* plays), whose title is 'The Old Warriors'. A *chigo* from the provincial temple of Sagami arrives at an inn in the town of Fujisawa, near Kamakura, accompanied by a servant. He is on the way to the capital. Hearing that the *chigo* is very pretty, the *wakashu*, that is to say the young men of the town, go to the town en masse, 'desiring the honour of being served sake by him'. (To be served sake by one's superior is thought of as a great honour.) To their great joy, and thanks to the innkeeper, they are allowed into the *chigo*'s room. The feast begins. But at that moment an old man comes and demands of the innkeeper that he too should be allowed to see the *chigo*, 'so as to comfort his old age'. The innkeeper refuses because the room is already overfull. The proud old man gets angry. He calls together his friends to throw out the young people, and they all go off the inn, each carrying his weapon!

At the moment when a fight between the young and the old men seems inevitable, however, the young men, following a plan of the *chigo*'s servant, leap into the arms of the old and embrace them. The old men find themselves to be, 'against all expectation, "*waka-zoku*-phile" '. (*Waka-zoku*, meaning young man, is a synonym of *wakashu*.) All retire, in couples, with a joyful air.

This obscene and comic play from the beginning of the 15th century is not only evidence of the provincial vogue for homosexuality, but also tells us that at that time two kinds of homoeroticism, '*shonin*-mania' (*shonin* or *shonen* being the current word for 'boy'), and '*wakazoku*-philia' were both fashionable. *Shonin*-mania is the love of boys from nine or ten to sixteen or seventeen years old; it is, of course, the love of the *chigo*. *Wakazoku*-philia designated the love of an older adult for *wakashu*, young men from seventeen or eighteen to about twenty-two or twenty-three years of age. It resembles more closely the homosexuality of our own day than the paedophile love for the *chigo*. However, with the change in the cultural tradition of homosexuality, it seems that these two kinds become one. At the same time, there was invented as designating the love-object a new compound word *chigo-wakashu*, which, shortened, became simply *wakashu*. Essentially, *wakashu* became the general term which covered both *chigo* and *wakashu* in its original sense. It is on the basis of this new definition that the word itself and the concept of *shudo* were formed and underwent development.

And so *shudo* spread gradually during the whole of this very troubled period, not only amongst the samurai, but also amongst the people. Nonetheless, for it to become really popular, we have to await the establishment of the new *bakufu* of Edo and the advent of the 'Great Three-Hundred-Year Peace of the Tokugawa', when the *kabuki*, a more recent and more popular theatre than the *no*, plays an important role in its dissemination.

'The Great Three-Hundred-Year Peace of the Tokugawa'

It was three great military leaders, Nobunaga, Hideyoshi and Ieyasu, who brought to an end the long period of civil war. Oda Nobunaga, perhaps the cleverest strategist of the three, pacified half of Japan but died a violent death, as has already been mentioned. It was Toyotomi Hideyoshi who completed the work left unfinished by the death of his master. The son of a poor peasant, he eventually achieved supreme power and ruled Japan as the regent of the Tenno. His

80

incredible life, known to us through his almost legendary biography, the *Taiko ki*, or 'Story (*ki*) of Great Regent (*taiko*)', is still an inspiration to Japanese boys. In the 'Loves of the Beautiful Bansaku' in section 2 of Chapter III, we were able to see in detail what *shudo* really was in Hideyoshi's time.

After the death of Hideyoshi, when his son Hideyori was still very young, there were internal problems in the government of the Toyotomi. The great lords formed two parties. Finally, in 1600, they engaged in the decisive battle of Sekigahara. This resulted in the establishment at Edo, by Tokugawa Ieyasu, head of the victorious party, of the new power called the Tokugawa *bakufu*, or more commonly, the *bakufu* of Edo. The regime established by Ieyasu was exceptionally stable. During the 265 years of the Edo period, there was not one serious revolt. There were only the peasant revolts which occasionally caused problems for the provincial lords. During this long peace, and in the isolation which the *bakufu* imposed on Japan by reducing its contact with foreigners, pure Japanese culture flourished. The sovereign popular entertainment throughout the whole 'Three-Hundred-Year Peace of the Tokugawa' was *kabuki*, which was born at the very beginning of the Edo period.

Women's *kabuki* and *wakashu kabuki*

It is generally accepted that the origins of *kabuki* lie in the women's dance companies which performed on stages on the banks of the river Kamo, which crosses Kyoto. This new form of theatre was a great sensation. It was enthusiastically welcomed everywhere, and at Edo in particular. *Kabuki* had a different attraction compared to *no*, for a number of reasons: it was a profane art, free of the patronage of the temples; it found its material in daily life, rather than in the classics; masks were never used; the physical attractions of the actors played an important role; and finally, one of its chief features was the presence of young girls dressed as boys. However, in 1629, the authorities put an end to this *onna kabuki*, or women's *kabuki*, forbidding women to go on stage. It was accused of corrupting public morality: the scenes were too erotic, and the actresses were often involved in prostitution.

After the banning of the *onna kabuki*, what took its place was the *wakashu kabuki*, where the actors were *wakashu*, young men (Ill. 17). When they appeared as a pretty *o-kosho* or page, gracefully clothed in a *furi-sode* (a robe with long kimono sleeves), the spectators found that the *shudo* hitherto reserved to the upper classes was now within their reach, and were madly enthusiastic. According to a document of 1658: 'They have produced a theatre called *wakashu kabuki* in which the dancers are young men. Many men were so enchanted by their charms that they ended up swearing their eternal love and becoming ill by seriously wounding their arms...' ('Tokaido meisho ki', or 'Beautiful Places on the Tokaido Road').

'Wounding their arms' means that at that time, lovers mixed their blood as a sign of their eternal love.

Here is another example from a book published in 1662: 'They got young men to sing and dance, and there were many rich men who were so carried away that they spent mad sums on them and end up in ruin. Their property disappeared as a thin covering of snow melts away beneath the rays of the spring sun' ('Edo meisho ki' or 'Beautiful Places in Edo').

It was not only the graceful costume of the *o-kosho*, but also the women's dress worn by the actors that so delighted the spectators. Here is a text written at the end of the 17th century: 'In the Kan'ei era (1624-29), men's *kabuki* was authorised. Young adolescents were dressed as women, and they looked like pretty young girls. There were so many libertines who fell in love with these transvestites that morals were gravely corrupted. At that time there was a beautiful young man named Shimada Man'nosuke. It was said of him in a poem:

> He seems to be a woman
> in the eyes of all the world,
> but he is nonetheless a man in reality.
> Man'nosuke, you are truly
> the androgynous Narihira![4]

Wagoto hajime, or 'The Origin of Things in Japan'

At that time the word *wakashu-gao*, meaning *wakashu*-face, expressing the beauty of a particular type of girl, was in fashion. The face of the adolescent boy, an androgyne face, was in fact the ideal of feminine beauty at that time. This shows to what an extent the *wakashu* of the *kabuki* had become an object of public admiration. The *wakashu kabuki*, however, was itself forbidden in 1652, on account of the corruption of public morals.

The evolution of *kabuki*
Thanks to the eager entreaties of those affected, the theatres were the next year given permission to reopen. What then appeared, however, was no longer the *wakashu kabuki*. All the actors had been forced by the government to cut off the *mae-gami*, the long locks at the forehead which were at that time the distinguishing mark of a young man. What had made the charm of the youth and

17. The *wakashu* of the *kabuki* theatre were much loved. (Supplied by M. Takeshi Kaneko, Tokyo.)

the beauty of the *wakashu* had been exactly this 'front hair', which often gave a young man's hair the appearance of a young girl's. A *wakashu* without his *mae-gami* was no longer a *wakashu*. He was, as they said at the time, no more than a peasant – a *yaro* (*ya-ro*, country-man). 'Finding that their beautiful *wakashu* were no longer *wakashu*, their admirers, it is said, wept tears of blood, through excess of grief' ('Edo meisho ki').[5]

The actors, however, did not give up in the face of this attack. They covered their foreheads with a violet kerchief, and thus found a way to make themselves as erotic as before and to remain the objects of homosexual love. This little violet cap was called '*yaro* hat', and *kabuki*, after these changes, *yaro kabuki*. The *kabuki* of our own day is itself essentially the *yaro kabuki*, because the actors are adult men (Ill. 18).

The transformation of the *wakashu kabuki* into the *yaro kabuki* had unexpected effects on its development. The working life of the actors became longer, no longer relying on the charm of the *mae-gami*, whereas the actors of the *wakashu kabuki* were generally at the height of their popularity at fifteen or sixteen years of age. It followed too that they would want to rely not only on their physical charms, but also to develop their skill as an end in itself. Finally, the development of the wig which followed on the loss of the 'front hair' made possible the development of the art of the *oyama*, a specialist in feminine roles. *Kabuki*, which had hitherto been no more than a form of suggestive music-hall, began to develop into an authentic theatrical form.

Yoshizawa Ayame: a master of the art of the *oyama*

It is in the Genroku era (1688-1703) that *kabuki* reaches theatrical perfection. The traditional civilisation of Japan attained its full flower in this period. In fact, while the great writer Ihara Saikaku (1642-93) was writing his masterpieces, among them the 'Glorious Tales of Homosexual Love',[6] Matsuo Basho (1644-94), the prince of Japanese poets, and Chikamatsu Monzaemon (1653-1724), a great dramatic author, were also at the height of their activity. *Ukiyo-e*, the Japanese print, although reaching its apogee in the Bunka and Bunsei eras (1804-30), was also beginning to develop. What fundamentally distinguishes the Genroku era from all previous periods is that its culture is not that of the ruling classes, but belongs to all.

Among the many famous actors who were working in this period, there was an *oyama* named Yoshizawa Ayame, born in the great merchant city of Osaka in the year 1673. He lost his father while very young, and became a courtesan to support himself, neither an exceptional nor a suspicious background for a

18. Famous actors of the Genroku period wearing the '*yaro* hat'. Kokan Taroji, Sawamura Kodenji, Suzuki Heishichi. (Illustrations of the 17th c., reproduced in *Nihon koten bungaku zenshu*, vol. 39, Shogaku-kan, Tokyo, 1973.)

actor. Such prostitution was considered a necessary stage in the career of an *oyama*. As his protector Gorosaemon was a great lover of *no*, the young *oyama* wanted, with his help, to learn the *no* dance. Rather than agree to Ayame's plans, Gorosaemon advised him to observe carefully the behaviour of real women and to make a great effort to express, in a realistic fashion, their movements and their manners. As he records in his book, 'Ayame's Notebook', a collection of personal observations on his art, it was as a result of this advice that he began to apply himself seriously to the art of *oyama*. He goes on: 'One cannot become an excellent *oyama* without living as a woman in everyday life. In fact, his masculinity betrays itself easily in him who makes an effort of will to become a woman on the stage. What is really important is everyday life...'

This principle of Ayame's, to be a woman even in everyday life, was followed by all the *oyama*. They always dressed as women, at home and in the street; the public accepted this behaviour. These customs even became one of the principal attractions of *kabuki*. Indeed, there was tacit approval for these transvestites to bathe at the public baths reserved for women, and not in those for men! The curious and special manners of the *oyama* disappeared gradually with the modernisation of Japanese society, above all with the Meiji restoration of 1868.

Yoshizawa Ayame claimed too, as against his predecessors, that the *oyama* should not plan to become a *tateyaku* and play men, even when his beauty should begin to fade: 'Hardly has an *oyama* decided that he will become a *tateyaku* than his art becomes altogether insipid' (ibid.).

What distinguishes the Japanese *oyama* from men playing women in the Elizabethan theatre is precisely this principle of Ayame's: an *oyama* should remain an *oyama* all his life. From this point of view, the *oyama* in *kabuki* are no longer mere substitutes for 'real women'. They will be obliged to pursue, throughout their lives 'the femininity that only men can bring into being'. It is thanks to this femininity of artifice, more 'real' than natural femininity, that *kabuki* escaped the fate of the English theatre where actors playing women disappeared towards the end of the 17th century. Today, it is not uncommon for *oyama* from *kabuki* to appear on the screen together with women, real actresses, and one is often surprised to see that they yield nothing in feminine charm, nor even in popularity. The flower of *kabuki*, this art and ideal of the *oyama*, was thus formed in the Genroku era, thanks to the effort and genius of Ayame and of a few other excellent players (Ill. 19). We wonder, certainly, why the *yaro kabuki*, where men played women, was finally authorised, while the women's *kabuki* where young girls were dressed as boys had been banned only thirty years before!

In our modernised societies, where women's beauty is so glorified, men dressed as women are considered ridiculous and dishonoured, while women remain charming even dressed as men. But in this period, men dressing as women was considered to be less dangerous than women dressing as men.

We will return again to this problem in Chapter V, where the relationship between the modernisation of society and the decline of the *shudo* will be considered from a theoretical point of view.

Shudo and the shoguns in the 17th century

What was the evolution of homosexual customs among the ruling class of samurai during this period?

The *bakufu* announced several times that it was forbidden for actors to be objects of homosexual activity. This prohibition, however, was not very strictly applied in reality, for the government had a weak spot. Its successive heads, the shoguns themselves, were well known for their homosexual tastes, and particularly the third, the shogun Iemitsu (1604-51). His reputation as a lover of young men even reached the countries of Europe, through the account of Franccois Callon (1600-73), the head of a Dutch company at Nagasaki:

> The present emperor (that is to say, the shogun) was not married when he came to the throne; he even lived a long time without women at all; the low opinion in which he holds them and the shameful inclination he has towards boys have always kept him from marriage; the Dayro (that is, the Tenno) sent him the two most beautiful girls of his country, so as to persuade him from this abomination, begging him to take as his wife or Midai (the Japanese for 'empress') the one who pleased him most; he chose one, whom he nonetheless did not frequent, living still in the same way... (translated into French by Melchisedec Thevenot in 1644).[7]

Later, however, having succeeded in having a child of a concubine, it is said that he loved women during the second half of his life.

Tsunayoshi, the fifth shogun, who reigned during the Genroku period, was also fond of young men, and for a long time ignored women. It is said that he always had about 150 young male concubines in his palace, among whom there were some who held real power when they reached adulthood, Yanagisawa Yoshiyasu (1658-1714), for example. At an advanced age, the shogun eventually began to frequent women, but it is said that he nonetheless remained homosexual until his death. Here is what a Korean ambassador (who came to Japan a little later, during the reign of Yoshimune, the eighth shogun), said about this fashion for homosexuality which affected all classes of the Japanese population:

> There are many male favourites who surpass young girls in beauty and attractiveness; they much exceed them, in their toilet especially, painting themselves with false eyebrows, making themselves up, dressing in coloured robes decorated with designs, dancing with fans; these beautiful young men are like flowers. King, noble, or rich merchant, there is no one who does not keep these beautiful young men... I have never heard of such a thing in other countries ('A Voyage across the Sea'). (See Ill. 20.)

Tacitly supported by the samurai class, the homosexual performance of *kabuki* was able to develop and eventually to reach its maturity. It served in its turn to popularise *shudo* among the people, and so it was in the Genroku period that the cultural tradition of homosexuality reached its Golden Age.

19. Four famous *oyama* of the Genroku period. (Illustrations of the 17th c., reproduced in *Nihon Koten Bungaku Zenshu*, vol. 39, Shogaku-kan, Tokyo, 1973.)

Ito Kodayu

Uemura Kichiya

Takii Yamasaburo

Tamagawa Shuzen

20. Young adolescent dancing with a fan. (From *Shin-yu ki*, reproduced in *Nihon shiso taikei*, vol. 60, Iwanami Shoten, Tokyo, 1976.)

2. Curious tales of the kagema

(this section is an extract from Juni'chi Iwata)

Today, a male prostitute is called a *kagema*.[8] In the Genroku period, when homosexuality was more fashionable than ever before, these prostitutes were generally called *yaro*, and the word *kagema* was applied only to a special kind. This change in terminology reflects a change in customs. Before the word *yaro*, the word *wakashu* was used, because there existed at that time the *wakashu kabuki*, whose actors were at the same time prostitutes. But *wakashu* had for a long time been the general term for a young man who belonged to the samurai class or to the bourgeoisie.

These '*wakashu* of the theatre' prostituted themselves so extensively that one might well ask whether it was a regular sideline for them. The world welcomed them with open arms and admired them greatly. At that time, a century of civil war had just come to an end, and Japanese society was not yet as refined as it would become. Some conducted themselves with great bravado, others dared to behave in a very childish manner. They were not condemned; on the contrary, they were often praised for their supposed naivety or ingenuousness. In such an atmosphere, for those who were in love with a young man, their principle might be a love 'at the risk of life itself'. Lovers swore eternal love, tatooing or cutting each other's arms or thighs so as to mix their blood.

At the beginning, this samurai custom became popular even among the admirers of the '*wakashu* of the theatre'. We find in a story of this period the most extreme examples: a samurai arrived from the provinces attends a performance and is profoundly affected by the beauty of a *wakashu*; he climbs onto the stage, cuts off his ear with his sword and offers it to this young man who has him under such a spell!

Even this kind of idiocy was sometimes applauded by the public. The authorities however were disturbed by this fashion, especially when it spread from the samurai to the popular classes. This is why the *bakufu* forbade the *wakashu kabuki*, considering it to be responsible for the corruption of public morals.

These young men, actors and prostitutes at the same time, then appeared in another form, the *yaro*, and from then on prostitutes were no longer called *wakashu*.

As actors and prostitutes, the *yaro* were in some sense the product of chance. All the young actors had to shave off the *mae-gami* (the front hair) so that the authorities would allow the theatres to reopen. The *bakufu* seems to have believed that in this way the charms of the *wakashu*, which had so affected the *kabuki* audience, could be diminished. Indeed, a *wakashu* without *mae-gami* was no longer a *wakashu*, but only a man, or more pejoratively, a peasant (*yaro*). The actors and theatre managers, however, attempted to get out of this difficult situation and eventually succeeded; having covered the shaved front part of the head with a piece of violet silk, the young actors became even more attractive than before! From then on, the violet silk would trouble the hearts of many spectators.

This silk crepe was named the '*yaro* hat', or 'violet hat'. From the 'Ukiyo soshi' (literally 'Sketchbooks of This World') and the 'Hyoban ki' ('Documents of Rumour'), which played the role of the newspapers of the present day, we can tell how much the actors' new costume was admired. In the Genroku period, male prostitutes were simply called *yaro*.

The real occupation of the *yaro* was of course to play in the theatres, or indeed to seem to do so. This was necessary so as not to upset the authorities. In reality they mostly appeared on the stage so that they might more easily be chosen by certain of the audience. As their primary profession was that of actor, it is no surprise that they should have been classified by skill in their art: *tayu-go*, *itatsuki*, etc. And it is natural too that these *yaro* as prostitutes should be hierarchically organised according to their rank as actors. A long apprenticeship was needed to become a professional actor. The future *yaro*, educated in the company from childhood on, were able to acquire a solid basis for their acting. They needed two kinds of apprenticeship, however, for they were intended to be both actors and prostitutes. We will speak later of this second apprenticeship. Apprentices sufficiently old might already have some experience in this field, even before they were ready to appear on the stage. They sometimes had walk-on parts, called '*shidashi ozei*', where actors were in short supply, but they were not yet true performers. They were however already expert in the second profession. It was they who were called, in those days, *kagema*. It is in this sense that I said at the beginning that the word *kagema* was only applied to a certain category of prostitutes.

The word *kagema*, however, had been known for long enough. Its etymology is 'shady (*kague*) room (*ma*)'. According to Mr Minakata Kumagusu,[9] this word is sometimes found in certain books of *haiku* (short poems in three lines of five, seven and five syllables successively, popular throughout the Edo period), older than those usually known. It was therefore employed before the Genroku period, and may have its origin in the monasteries.

21. *Wakashu.* A beautiful *wakashu* and his servant. (From the *Kin-mo zu-i,* or 'Illustrated dictionary to enlighten the mind', 1666.)

22. *Oku-gosho* and their servants. They were a superior *o-kosho* who waited upon the shogun. (From *Ukiyo no tsuzuki,* 1682.)

23. Two *wakashu* and a cock. (From *Shimabara kyogen ukiyo no tsuzuki*, 1682.)

24. 'Actors.' Two of them wear the *yaro* cap. (From the *Yakusha hyoban ki*, or 'Record of the actors', 1704.)

At the time when the *yaro* enjoyed a great popularity there existed other kinds of prostitutes, because homosexuality in general was very fashionable. *Kagema* were one type, of course. Another type was called *tobi-ko*; they were regarded as less elegant than the *yaro* or the *kagema*. These were the ones who, despite their apprenticeship, were unable to appear on stage in the capital and were sent to perform in the provinces. They were a kind of travelling player. They extended their sphere of activity further and further until it covered nearly all the Japanese towns. The *kongo*, a kind of servant who looked after the *yaro* in every way, also went with the *tobi-ko* in their arduous travels. Among the *tobi-ko* there would also be a few *yaro* no longer highly regarded on account of their age or their lack of skill in their art, or even actors who were unable to remain in the capital because of other problems.

These *yaro* reduced to the condition of *tobi-ko* were often thirty or even forty years old. Such *tobi-ko*, despite their age, would steal the hearts of monks and rich country-dwellers by dressing up as young adolescents.

The *tobi-ko* had a difficult enough life. Quite commonly, their *kongo*, on whom they relied, would deceive them and end up running away having spent all the money that the poor prostitutes had earned. On the other hand, it often happened that a *tobi-ko* would become very closely involved with his *kongo*, especially when provincial clients wanted to make him do hateful things. In fact, they often loved each other with all their hearts. When the poor *tobi-ko* left his client and returned tired to his lodging late at night, the *kongo* would have prepared his supper and would cover his beloved with clothes warmed by his own body. When a client tried to force him to drink, his *kongo* would protect him, saying: 'Sir, he cannot drink a drop!' Here was the modest consolation allowed to the poor wandering prostitute...

In the Kyoho era (1716-36), the fashion for *yaro* and even for homosexuality itself disappeared. The shogun at this time was Tokugawa Yoshimune. He was very capable, and he also practised a policy of economy so as to restore the finances of the state. The financial condition of the state was stabilised and there began the period of peace known as the 'Peace of Kyoho'. In this tranquility, the life of the people improved, as is attested by the number of persons visiting the great Shinto temple of Ise, which was greater in the Kyoho period than in the whole of the rest of the Edo.[10] But the shogun Yoshimune greatly detested debauchery. If a man was rich enough to afford it, he had nonetheless to abstain, so as not to upset the authorities. During the great peace of Kyoho, one had to be very discreet in taking one's pleasure with women; it was even more impossible to throw oneself into homosexual pleasure, chiefly because it was regarded as being

25. One of the actors is wearing the *yaro* cap. (From *Shimabara kyogen ukiyo no tsuzuki.*)

26. Celebrated actors of the Bunka era (1803-18). The one with the *mae-gami* is perhaps a *kagema*. (From *Bukyoku senrin*, a book on music and the dance, 1815.)

still more luxurious. In fact, it was those who had sufficiently taken their pleasure with women who had often ended up with this other love. It is not surprising then that the *yaro* disappeared, at least from social visibility, and that the fashion for homosexuality should have gone with them.

In this way, even the word *yaro* was forgotten. Very shortly afterwards came the years when the civilisation of the Edo period reached its height. These were the eras of Horeki (1751-63), Meiwa (1764-71), An'ei (1772-80) and Temmei (1781-89), during which culture was the most refined of the three Tokugawa centuries. They can be compared to the Senna era (1119-25) of the So period in China or to the rococo age of Louis XV. In these years there appeared numerous *tsu-jin*, elegant persons who were well acquainted with the *demi-monde*. They held all things up to ridicule. There certainly must have been a great deal of rancour and discontent beneath the surface of society, but in appearance, people enjoyed a long period of tranquility. Many comic poets were engaged in mocking the world. Many licentious stories were published, often full of pictures and drawings, and they were called *share-hon* (= book of elegance) or *kibyo-shi* (= yellow cover). *Iki* (chic) and *tsu* (knowledge of the world) were much appreciated. The brothel districts became prosperous once more. In this new climate, homosexuality made a comeback. Male prostitution, which had hitherto been practised only in secret by actors, became the overt occupation of specialists. There appeared many establishments offering homosexual pleasures to the public. Homosexuality became as popular as it had been before. The new centre for these entertainments was Edo, in place of Kyoto and Osaka in the Genroku period. The genius Hiraga Gen'nai[11] made propaganda for these tastes by writing many guides.

In this period, however, the word *yaro* had almost disappeared. There were certainly other words which meant a male prostitute: *iroko*, *kagueko* etc. But it was *kagema* which was generally employed; it became the generic term for a prostitute. Even today one sometimes talks of a *kagema*, while the word *wakashu*, as a general term for a beautiful young man, has fallen into disuse. But *kagema* is used to designate the strange vagabonds who haunt the darkened parks.

How did one become a *kagema*? There is an abundant literature that answers our question. Through the whole history of the *yaro* and the *kagema*, what is written is pretty much the same. According to a book which appeared in the first year of Shotoku (1711), the future *yaro* was treated as follows:

> When he is small, he is only given clothes already worn, and he is treated much more severely than any other craftsman's apprentice. He must often do the shopping, look after the children, chop wood for

the fire etc. If any time is left to him, he must learn how to write, writing in the ashes. He certainly wants his sleep...

This might be a slight exaggeration, but it seems to me undeniable that the condition of the future *yaro* or *kagema* was pretty miserable. The small boys who after such sorry years would become *kagema* were pretty children from poor families. In general, they were 'bought' very young and brought up by the owner of a 'house of *kagema*' (Ill. 35).

The following extract, a passage from a *share-hon* which appeared in the Kyoho era, tells of the actor's apprenticeship:

> It is at the age of eight years that he begins to learn to play the *shamisen* (the traditional Japanese three-stringed guitar, see Ills. 26 and 34). The little boy, woken before daybreak, applies himself to it through the whole day. The exercise of the white frosty night, called *kan-biki* (playing in the cold), and the special lesson during the dog-days were particularly arduous. His employer gives the poor child no rest. When he is a little older, he accompanies a *wakashu* as far as the wings and tries to take him as a model for his acting. The day finally comes when he makes his debut on the stage. He first of all plays the role of a *kaburo*, a prostitute's little servant, more appropriate to his age (Ill. 35). Nonetheless, when he returns from the theatre, he must receive his clients.

A *kagema*'s apprenticeship was certainly not easy. Of course, from a certain age, the future *kagema* was no longer given minor tasks: he no longer had to do the shopping or look after a child, but he then had to take taxing lessons in the guitar and in dancing which would see him fall down with fatigue. Hardly has he more or less succeeded than he begins to receive clients, monks or laymen, nobles or commoners. That is the making of a *kagema*.

In the 'Glorious Tales of Homosexual Love' by Ihara Saikaku, we find many other words than *kagema* used to designate a prostitute. This author seems to call all kinds of prostitute the same thing, *ko-domo*, child. However, the *yaro*, the *kagema* and the *tobi-ko* are all to be distinguished from each other, not only by their rank but also by their external appearance. The most notable difference lies in the fact that while the *kagema* wore beautiful *mae-gami*, the *yaro* had only the 'yaro cap' in place of the *mae-gami* which they had unhappily lost since the prohibition of the *wakashu kabuki*. This must be because the *kagema* as such did not

27. 'The lord.' A great lord and his *o-kosho* (From the *Kinmo zu-i*.)

28. 'Yaro.' (From *On'na dai-gaku takarabako*, 1733.)

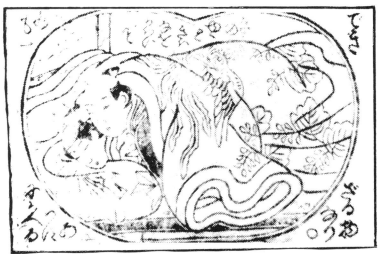

appear on the stage. We see in certain illustrations of this period some persons who have the *mae-gami* among those who wear the *yaro* cap (in Ill. 26 for example). These are the *kagema*. One finds, too, in the 'Collection of Legal Prohibitions of the Tokugawa Period', a proclamation of the second year of the Genroku era which speaks of 'those who do not appear on stage and who may wear the *mae-gami*...' This phrase clearly shows that the *kagema* wore the *mae-gami*.

The *tobi-ko* sent to the provinces also wore the *mae-gami*; this can be seen in certain paintings of the period, for example in an illustration to the second volume of Saikaku's 'Life of a Friend of Voluptuousness' (Ill. 4 5).

One cannot say that all the *tobi-ko* arranged their hair in the same way; there were among them many *yaro* who had left the theatres of the cities. In the proclamation mentioned above, 'travelling *yaro*' are distinguished from 'theatre *yaro*'. They travelled from one province to another as actors, prostituting themselves as they went. In the 'Secret Stories of the Kibi Country, Wherein to Regret the Past' there is an item which illustrates the lives of the travelling *yaro*. In the second year of the Tenwa era (1682) a *yaro* called Yoshida Rokunosuke came from Osaka and prostituted himself often in the town of Miyauchi (in the province of Bichu). All those who had relations with him were questioned by the authorities and the actor-prostitute was exiled from the province. According to another document, when the *tobi-ko* went to work in a town where homosexual prostitution was strictly forbidden, they went in big wicker baskets so as to escape observation. This is a description from a collection of anecdotes, which seems a little suspect, however:

> I think I have seen this boy somewhere before. Ah! I remember now.
> It's surely the lad who always had a child to look after. He was often
> sent shopping. How he used to like cheap cakes!

By the time he was the subject of such an observation, he would have already have become a 'professional'. The urchin who used to amuse himself by keeping a mouse, or setting a dog upon a cat, is now dressed in a long and elegant kimono. He walks along with a coquettish air, seeming to have forgotten his miserable past. He conducts himself with elegance, as if he were a nobleman's bastard. More and more experienced in his 'trade', he knows its every artifice. To provincial clients, he is all compliments, though he makes fun of them to himself and plans to diddle them of as much money as possible. This is the way of all those who prostitute themselves, men and women. With his clients, he seems a real

29. *'Wakashu'.* (From *Nanshoku jussun no kagami*, 1687.)

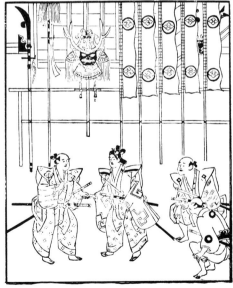

30. 'Samurai dress.' A samurai and a young man both wearing the samurai costume called *kamishima*. The two men on the right are their servants. (From Saikaku's *Bushido denrai ki* ('Stories of the samurai spirit', 1687.)

innocent. He pretends not to know what is going on in the world. he says that he doesn't know the price of a bundle of firewood or a sheaf of toilet-paper. Clients really like this. It is a feature which he has in common with the *mie* (outward honour) of the geisha of the present day.

Nevertheless, these habits of the *kagema*, which struck observers as charming, were only a way of gaining a living. Far from being satisfied in their coquetry, they lived always in very sorry circumstances. They dared not eat what they wanted, for fear of being seen by their master. They had to take lessons in art though they were hungry, they had to write love-letters to clients, though they might detest them. If they wanted to stay longer with a favourite client, their *kongo* would interrupt to take them to the next. This one is perhaps a drinker and will force him to drink all the time. The poor boy has to drink as if he hadn't already had enough with the last, and shower this other with smiles and signs of affection as if he were the first client of the evening. Moreover, the essentials of his work are difficult, and often painful. He is eventually allowed to return to his room, almost dead with fatigue. And yet, he might soon be called out to receive yet another client! It's only towards the end of the night that he will be allowed to sleep, but he will have to get up early for his lessons...

In such circumstances, it is not surprising that the *kagema*'s principal concern was to gain some pocket-money.

'The *ko-domo* of those days were really innocent. They never asked their clients for money, even after they had been several times...,' wrote Ihara Saikaku, in Volume V of the 'Glorious Tales of Homosexual Love', talking about the advantages of the time of the *wakashu kabuki*. As the distinction was established between the actors, called *butai*(= stage)-*ko* and the *kagema*, professional prostitutes, the *kagema* lost the innocence of the *wakashu* of the old days. They often asked for money from their regular clients. It often happened that to escape fatigue, and especially pain, they had recourse to the clever ruse of intercrural coitus. Their only concerns were now to make as much money as possible and to escape from the problems of *coitus a tergo* by every possible lie and deception. In the client's eyes this must have been unforgivable. But for the poor prostitutes, this became their way of life.

One might think that these young men, living in such miserable circumstances, would wish to escape them as soon as possible. I can't help being surprised that there were many of them who continued this life until they were well grown up. In general, there was an age limit for male prostitutes somewhere between eighteen and twenty. After passing this limit, the *yaro* applied themselves, as actors, to the art of the theatre. The *kagema*, however, and the

31. 'A Noble and his *chigo*.'
The small figure on the
right is perhaps the noble's
boy-servant. (From *Sugata-
e hyakunin isshu*, 1695.)

32. *Yamabushi* and *chigo*.
See remarks on *yamabushi*
on p. 70. (From *Sugata-e
hyakunin isshu*, 1695.)

33. *Kaburo*, a girl who acts
as a (female) prostitute's
servant. (From *Kinmo zu-i*
or 'Illustrated dictionary to
enlighten the mind',
1666.)

unskilful *yaro*, had no future on the stage, but due to their apprenticeship from childhood they could no longer become merchants, for example, and many of them were obliged to remain prostitutes and to try and preserve their youthful looks by artifice. In Volume V of his 'Glorious Tales...', Saikaku remarks: 'It is strange that these *yaro* dress as *wakashu* and give themselves to men, even up to the age of 34 or 35.'

The most extreme example was that of a *kagema* called Hagino Yaegiri. By reason of his profound love for a man, he never wished to know a woman, and even after the age of 60 he never changed his *wakashu* dress. Nor did his partner forget this *kagema*, and he always slept with him until they were very old. This rather excessive example is to be found in a book entitled *Fumoto no iro* (literally: Colour at the foot of a mountain), which appeared in 1769. There were many *kagema* who willingly remained true to their calling, enjoying the secret pleasures of the profession despite the general difficulties of their situation, even when youth had passed.

While in the Genroku period the fashionable centres of homosexual pleasure were Kyoto and Osaka, these curious blossoms the *kagema* were at their most flourishing, at Edo especially, from the Meiwa era to the Tempo reform (1841). The *kagema* of Edo, at this time, openly had both men and women as clients. To explain this phenomenon, we must take into account the existence of the numerous ladies in waiting who worked in the harem of the Edo palace, where no man was allowed to enter. We should note that many bourgeois widows then began to imitate these ladies. Many satirical haiku testify to the indiscriminate indulgence in these pleasures by ladies of the harem. Many verses too were written about the widows. It seems that the *kagema* who served the widows were for the most part fairly old. Here is an example:

> The widows get those
> Soon will show themselves monsters
> On Yoshi-cho street.[12]

As regards clients of the other sex, it seems that a good many of them were monks. Prints and illustrations of this period show us that at that time most of the *kagema* of Edo were in the habit of dressing up as girls (Ill. 46). Among them were a happy few who, profoundly loved by a priest of high rank, would be able to live their whole life in ease, receiving a portion of a temple's revenue, or keeping a tea-house or restaurant, under the protection of their old lover...

All this came to an end with the Tempo reform of 1842-43, which forbade

34. 'The famous *kagema Moritomo Sakon.*' *(From Yaro daishi*, 1668.)

35. 'House of the *yaro*.' An establishment which employs *yaro*. They gene-rally lived there from childhood. Here, a *yaro* is going out, perhaps to go on stage or to meet a client. (From *Furyu kyoku shamisen*, 1703.)

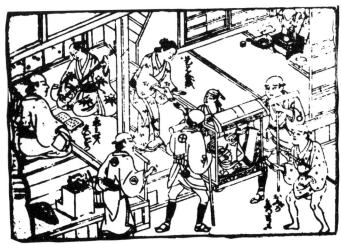

'tea-houses for pleasure' with *kagema*. It is true, of course, that these *kagema* tea-houses continued secretly to offer their particular pleasures, perhaps under the protection of great temples. In any event, the Meiji restoration, which was a great blow to Buddhism, finally brought about the disappearance of the male prostitutes. The word *kagema* thus fell into disuse; it was only heard in the tales of old men.

And yet it is very curious that since the Taisho era (1912-16), strange people have begun to haunt the hidden corners of Tokyo and Osaka, and they are now called *kagema*. These are not elegant; they are only vagabonds who prostitute themselves in the darker corners of the parks. It is incredible that they should have been given the name of the *kagema* of the Edo period, who were, no doubt about it, most elegant and graceful! If by chance you do not know the history, and seeing the *kagema* of today, believe that there existed such people in other times, I will remind you that the *kagema* of old were as charming and elegant in body as they were in their dress.

(end of extract from Jun'ichi Iwata)

36. 'The Feast.' A homo-
sexual scene from Saika-
ku's 'Life of a lover of
pleasure'.

37. '*Butai-ko, kage and tamago*.' The *butai-ko* (right), *kage* (= *kagema*), and
the *tamago* (a young boy not yet entered upon the life of an actor or
kagema) welcoming two clients, a monk and a samurai. The *tamago*
wears the *mae-gami*, but strangely, the *kagema* (next to the *butai-ko*) is
wearing the *yaro* cap. (From *Yaro kinuburi*.)

38. *'Jo-ton.'* One of the positions for anal intercourse. (From *Kinmo zu-i.*)

39. 'Monks' feast.' There are two monks and a *yaro*. (From Saikaku's 'Glorious tales of homosexuality'.)

40. 'A temple *o-kosho.*' A page who serves the monk at the temple. Unlike the *chigo* in the monasteries before the 16th century, he is dressed as a samurai *wakashu*. (From 'Glorious tales...')

V: *Shudo* or the Way of Adolescents

1. *The idea of* shudo

The idea of *shudo* before the 17th century

What has been described in the previous chapter is only one side of the coin. Aside from its sensual aspect, *shudo* was particularly developed by the samurai as an idea and as an ideal, that is to say, as a 'way'. We should note that its morality, its 'spirituality' even, were already stressed in the text in which the word *shudo* is found for the first time.

Lamenting that the *shudo* 'way' was being corrupted, Ijiri Chusuke passionately argued in 1482 that the the *shudo* ideal had existed 'in past times':

> In our empire of Japan, this way flourished from the time of the great Master Kobo particularly. And in the abbeys of Kyoto and Kamakura ... and in the world of the nobles and warriors, lovers would swear perfect and eternal love, relying on no more than their mutual goodwill. Whether their partners were noble or common, rich or poor, was absolutely of no importance. Consequently, some abandoned their property or lost their rank as a result of their passion, while others gained a fine position or acquired a name thanks to their love. But in all these cases they were greatly moved by the spirit of this way. This way must be truly respected and it must never be permitted to disappear.
> *The Essence of the Jakudo*, 1482.[1]

Such an attitude, criticising the present in the name of an 'ideal which once existed', is also found in the 'Introduction to the *Wakashu* of the Past and Present', written about a century later by Hosokawa Yusai, a famous general and *arbiter elegantiae* of the Nobunaga era: 'These celebrated persons are called *o-wakashu*,[2] and yet we find among them only one or two who know the ancient way, the

109

manner and rule of conduct of a *wakashu*. It is to make the old *jakudo* live again and to transmit it to posterity that I have written this Introduction.' In every way to criticise the current situation in relation to an ideal past is a kind of classicism not confined to Japan, but common to all traditional societies. On reading these passages we find them a little strange, however, for we have already seen that *shudo* was constituted as a way at a relatively late date. Do these reproaches addressed to the *shudo* of this time signify that the *shudo* ideal was never in fact realised?

What is the concrete content of the 'old way', the idea of *shudo*? According to the two works of the poet Sogi (1421-1502) entitled 'The Ethic of the *Chigo*' and 'Manners of the *Wakashu*', the qualities of the *wakashu* and the necessary conditions for becoming one were as follows:

1. To have a pure and simple heart.
2. To be both tender and noble.
3. When one is courted, even if the admirer is not very pleasing, one may not fail to respond to his passion. Nor may one be capricious.
4. One must love study, and especially the composition of   poetry.
5. One must not forget that the *wakashu* too grows old. To have been loved provides happy memories for one's old age.

This is the whole of the poet's advice to the young men of his time, and we cannot help but find it a little lacking in detail. Even in Hosokawa's 'Introduction', written eighty years later, soul and compassion are insisted upon as ideal qualities of the *wakashu*, and these concepts have no concrete elaboration. It seems likely that in these centuries the idea of *shudo* had not yet been properly formulated. We will therefore look now at the works of the early Edo period.

The idea of *shudo* during the Edo period

The *Shin-yu-ki*[3] or 'Book for the friends of the soul', which appeared in 1643 and offered guidance to *wakashu* from a Buddhist point of view, also lays the stress on 'soul' and on 'compassion':

> There are few beautiful young men who have soul. This confirms the proverb that beauty is in general soulless. He who is born infirm may perhaps have been beautiful in his previous life and yet did not respond to his admirer. Such physical deformity is the result of a lack

110

of soul in a previous life. If you remain without soul all through your youth, which is truly precious and irreversible, you will commit many sins and will surely be punished in your future life. Even when you are unable to take him who loves you into your heart, you should try and make *giri* (obligation)[4] your rule of conduct.

Essentially, he insists that *shudo* should conform with the idea of humanity conceived from a Buddhist point of view (Ill. 41).

'Obligation' is thus considered, together with 'soul' and 'compassion', as a foundation of *shudo*. We may find in Ihara Saikaku's *Buke giri monogatari* (literally, 'Samurai duty stories') an example of the high praise given to *shudo* governed by *giri*. This is the story:

The page Gorokichi, the favourite of a shogun, was so beautiful that the flowers of Kyoto would have paled before him. One day, by chance, he heard news of his old lover who had left him of his own free will so as to be no obstacle to his advancement. The old man was in the capital, not far away, and yet Gorokichi, so fiercely loved by his master, was not able to go and see him. Faced with this situation the tenderhearted young man fell ill of sadness.

He called his good friend Muranosuke to his bedside and said to him: 'Dear Muranosuke, when I am dead, seek out this old man and love him in my place!' The faithful Muranosuke promised him this and Gorokichi was able to die with a smile. After a long search, Muranosuke discovered the old man. His face was corrupted and decayed. He was more than sixty years old. To love this man was repulsive to Muranosuke, and yet he had to perform what he had promised to his dead friend.

'Dear stranger,' said the faithful young man, 'as he lay dying, our friend Gorokichi asked me to find you and to love you in his place. Love me then!'

First of all, very surprised at this proposal, the old man, naturally enough, did not accept his love. But finally, touched by his fidelity, he agreed to accept it. They promised to be lovers and friends for all their lives. Muranosuke visited the old man every evening. When the story became known, the whole world praised Muranosuke's conduct and his faithful love for the old man. He was not at all in love with him, but he kept him as his lover, so as to fulfil his promise, that is to say, for the sake of *giri*.

According to the *Inu tsurezure* ('A dog's idle hours') of 1653, *shudo* is above all the foundation of the excellence of daily life:

41. An illustration from the *Shin-yu ki*. A *wakashu* and his lover (*nenja*) hold hands. (Reproduced in *Nihon shiso taikei*, vol. 60, Iwanami Shoten, Tokyo, 1976.)

It is natural for a samurai to make every effort to excel with pen and sword. Beyond that, what is important to us is not ever to forget, even to our last moment, the spirit of *shudo*. If we should forget it, it will not be possible for us to maintain the decencies, nor gentleness of speech, nor the refinement of polite behaviour.

Indeed, the author discovers in *shudo* a way which surpasses that of everyday morality and says:

If you pray for happiness in future life, you must learn the teachings of the Buddha. If you learn the teachings of the Buddha and expect to achieve Awakening, you will surely practise *shudo*. For this way is really like that of the true Awakening, in that we may give ourselves wholly to it.

It is the 'soul' which is the foundation of *shudo*. Insisting in this way on the morality and the spirituality of *shudo* sometimes leads to the doctrine that the features and external appearance of the *wakashu* are only of secondary importance. The author of the *Danshoku ni rin no sho* ('Book of the two moralities of homosexuality', 1665) says, for example, 'We call *wakashu* with pure souls "excellent *wakashu*".The goodness or badness of a *wakashu* reside not in his appearance but in his soul.'

When the *wakashu*'s morality is insisted upon, one naturally ends up discussing the qualities of the true *nenja*,[5] the adult who loves the *wakashu*. According to the *Nanshoku jussun no kagami* ('A ten-inch mirror for homosexuality', 1687), whose first part is entirely devoted to the discussion of the ideal *nenja*, it is the *nasake* and the *giri* (the soul and the feeling of obligation) of the *wakashu* which make homosexual relations possible. So, in order to reward the *wakashu* for his *giri*, the *nenja* is duty-bound to see to his education. 'It is a grave fault not to teach a *wakashu* to distinguish between the true and the false. This must never be forgotten.' 'If a *wakashu* is unreasonable, we can imagine the soul of his lover.' He who cannot educate his beloved is not fit to practise *shudo*. We may conclude then, setting aside for a moment the question of its practical realisation, that after a long period of development, the Japanese tradition of homosexuality finally reached the level of the erotic pedagogy of Ancient Greece (Ill. 41).

42. '*Shudo*, an ornament of the warrior-class.' (From *Nanshoku yamaji no tsuyu*, which appeared in the Ganbun era (1736-41). New edition, with a commentary by Omura Shage, Nichirinkaku, Tokyo, 1980.)

The way of the samurai and the way of adolescents
A mysterious book, entitled *Hagakure* ('A life hidden behind the leaves'), appeared at the beginning of the 18th century. It is a collection of memories and reflections on morality by an old samurai of a province of Kyushu, intended to illustrate the true *bushi-do* or 'way of the samurai'. Although this book is well enough known and indeed considered dangerous on account of its supposed admiration for death, it is today no longer read. Some, however, like Mishima, do appreciate it, admire it even, seeing it as an expression not only of the samurai spirit at its most pure, but also of an eternal truth of human nature. This book provides the best example of the essential relationship between the two ways, the 'way of the samurai' and the 'way of youth'.

The ideal love is unknown and hidden in the heart
Here is a passage from Yamamoto Jocho (1649-1719) which clearly shows its author's idea of love:

> I believe that the ultimate ideal love is the unknown love hidden in the depths of the heart. This is because once it comes to the light of day, our love can become less pure and less passionate, and thus less noble. To die having all our life kept our passion secret, this is the true essence of love.

It should be noticed that in Japan such a 'platonic' attitude is never found in the heterosexual world. For the author, and for the readers of his time, 'love' always meant love of a young man. Seeing the word *koi* (love) all the way through the book, readers of our own day often confuse it with the love of women; this shows how ignorant are modern Japanese of the intimate connection which exists between *bushido* and *shudo*.

Examples of this connection are given in another passage in which Jocho explains the principles and etiquette of *shudo*. He first of all advises the boys:

> There is a proverb: a virtuous woman does not marry twice. It is the same for you *wakashu*. You must have only one lover in your life; otherwise there would be no difference between you and prostitutes or worse. It is truly a shame for a samurai... If you have had relations with your *nenja* for five years or so and you have found him to be really loyal, you must then put your trust in him completely. Because he is the person for whom you sacrifice your life, you really must see into his heart...

Then Jocho gives similar advice to the older men: 'You also, as I have already explained, you must really see into the heart of your *wakashu*. And even if it seems difficult to win his heart, you will succeed, I am sure, if only you concentrate on this for five or six years, at the risk of your life.' He ends his discourse as follows: 'Homosexual pleasure must never be pursued at the same time as pleasure with women. Moreover, what is really important is to practise the martial arts. It is only in this way that the *shudo* becomes *bushido*'.

The way of the samurai is the way of beauty
How can *shudo* become *bushido*? What is essential to the union of the two ways? Here we enter a little into the domain of psychology. Modern historians, without exception, believe that the popularity of homosexuality was simply the consequence of supposed restrictions on the freedom of sexual relations between the sexes. They say, in short, that *shudo* represents only a 'situational' homosexuality such as is found everywhere, in the army, in religious communities and in prison. This interpretation can certainly be made of the love of the *chigo* in the world of the monks, but as regards the love of young men in the world of the samurai, the real reasons seem to me to lie much deeper and must take account of a certain psychological structure.

Certain other passages of the *Hagakure* point us in the right direction:

'One should always carry rouge and powder with one,' advises Jocho. 'After rising in the morning, or after sobering up, we sometimes find that we do not look very good. In such a case we should take out the rouge and put it on.' These samurai of the Sengoku era used to perfume their hair with incense and they brushed their nails every morning. More, they were in the habit of putting on a light make-up before going into battle. They took care that their own faces should not, even in death, appear disagreeable in the eyes of the enemy. Everywhere in his work, Jocho talks of the importance of 'appearances'.

Here we find ourselves face to face with the essence of *bushido* considered as an 'aesthetic'. In a nutshell, the way of the samurai boils down to a practical philosophy which teaches how one may be 'beautiful' in death. As 'a samurai must prepare himself anew for death every morning and every evening,' the aesthetic of death can become, at the same time, an aesthetic of life. *Bushido*, at least in its most refined manifestation, can become, as a result, not only the philosophy of a beautiful death but also that of a beautiful life. Such a philosophy cannot fail to make its followers more or less narcissistic. We should remember too that there exists, according to certain psychoanalysts, a profound relationship between narcissism and the love of death. One might then predict, if this psychoanalytic doctrine is true, that the samurai will choose as a 'sexual object' a person who resembles him – a person of his own sex. In fact, according to Freud, it is precisely this narcissism that is one of the causes of homosexuality. In this case the samurai loved beautiful young men not because these latter resembled young girls, but because the youths resembled what they themselves had been during adolescence.

2. The sexuality of shudo

Shudo and bisexuality

There remain certain psycho-sociological problems, the most important of which is surely that of the relationship between *shudo* and heterosexuality. Were those who loved and practised *shudo* in Jocho's sense exclusively homosexual, considered from the psychological point of view?

We should note first of all that in the society of the Edo period, especially among the samurai, only the Buddhist religious were free to remain unmarried. In fact, all the lovers of *shudo* mentioned in this chapter, including Jocho, were married without exception and fulfilled their obligation to produce descendants. The future samurai is loved by adult men up to the age of majority; then, he loves adolescents younger than he is, and finally, a few years later, he sets up house with a wife. This seems to have been the common custom of the samurai of the time.

Was there some psychological necessity in this half-obligatory passage from homosexuality to heterosexuality? Were these samurai who loved young men forced to marry, as are certain homosexuals in present-day Japan, or did this 'conversion' indeed have a psychological necessity?

Certain documents seem to provide a clear answer to the question. In the fifth volume of the *Five Women in Love*,⁶ one of the masterpieces of the great Saikaku, the author presents the life of a man from the province of Satsuma, a centre of provincial *shudo*,⁷ and this life demonstrates precisely a 'conversion from homosexuality to heterosexuality.'

Gengobei was 'a handsome man, much given to sensual love' , yet 'He arrived at his twenty-sixth year without having had the least intercourse with the delicate sex. For a long time, he had had a lively affection for a young man' (Ill. 43). However, after the latter's unexpected death, he renounced the world and set out on a pilgrimage. Now there was a very pretty girl called O-Man who was

43. During a rainy night,
Gengobei and his beloved
Hachijuro play the flute
together. (From 'Five
women in love', vol. 4, ch.
1, reproduced in *Nihon
koten bungaku taikei*, vol.
47, Iwanami shoten,
1957.)

44. Gengobei and his
beloved O-man. They give
open-air theatrical performances to gain a living.
(From 'Five women in
love', vol. 4, ch. 5. op. cit.)

very much in love with Gengobei and 'had sent him many letters to tell him of the torment in her heart,' but had not ever received a reply. Hearing of Gengobei's departure, 'She cut her hair in the correct manner... and cleverly dressed herself up as the perfect young man. Then she set out secretly.' Eventually, she succeeded in sharing her loved one's bed. Gengobei discovered that she was a woman, but 'faced with such a sincere confession of love', he accepted her love, saying: 'Between the pleasure one has in a man, and that which one obtains with women, there is no difference.' He returns to the lay world and ends by marrying O-Man (Ill. 44). I cannot help thinking that behind this story there are many Gengobeis. (According to certain documents of the period, popular songs about this character were in fashion from 1671, fifteen years before the publication of Saikaku's *Five Women in Love*).

Saikaku's best-known work is perhaps the *Koshoku ichidai otoko*, or 'Life of a friend of pleasure', in which the author describes the life of a dandy called Yonosuke (Ill. 45). He is often regarded as a representative of a Japanese Don Juan, but we notice in the novel that this Don Juan was in reality bisexual rather than heterosexual. 'Of the total of 3,742 women and 725 young men that Yonosuke had loved up to the fifty-fourth year of his life, he had written them all down in his diary.' This is one of the passages which show his bisexuality and his astounding sensual appetite. Not just Saikaku's characters, but the actual dandies of the time, were in reality bisexual. It is probable that the spread of *shudo* offered suitable conditions for the development of that bisexuality which, as Freud says, is proper to human nature. As regards exclusive homosexuals, we may be fairly certain that there were less then than there are in our own day.

Sexual practice in *shudo*

How was *shudo* practised at the level of sexual behaviour? In the case of the love of *chigo* within the walls of the monastery, it was a matter of anal intercourse exclusively. This is demonstrated by the whole literature, in which we find no document which suggests fellatio, mutual masturbation or intercrural coitus. There is nothing surprising in this, for most of the monks who practised pederasty, it seems to me, were originally of heterosexual rather than homosexual orientation.

Even in the centuries of the *wakashu* we find a similar situation. No text alludes to other practices than anal intercourse, while very many stories, articles and essays talk, sometimes too frankly, of *shiri* or 'arse'. This too can be explained without difficulty. The kernel of homosexual culture was for centuries always pederasty in its original sense, that is to say the love of an older man for an

45. A homosexual scene from Saikaku's 'Life of a lover of pleasure'. A boy invites travellers into the 'tobi-ko house', a sort of homosexual bordello. (Reproduced in Nihon koten bungaku taikei, vol. 47, Iwanami Shoten, Tokyo, 1957.)

adolescent, and it is not surprising that the pederasts preferred anal intercourse, for relations rather like the heterosexual were easily established between the older man and the younger. We find in certain documents, however, evidence of homosexual relationships which were not pederastic; the love between grown men, for example, depicted in the *no* play 'Matsumushi' (the name of an insect rather like the grasshopper), and the love of two pages of the same age in some of Saikaku's works. But throughout the history of Japanese homosexuality, it is only pederasty in the strict sense which is accorded a social or cultural value. Between two grown men, or two pages, there may have been sexual behaviour other than anal intercourse. Writers, however, found nothing important to say about such behaviour, nor may they even have known of its existence.

There are decisive differences between the *shudo* and present-day homosexuality in Japan and in Western countries, where the love of adolescents no longer plays an essential role.

3. The Decline of Shudo and Modern Japanese Homosexuality

Decline, renaissance and eventual death of *shudo*

The final aspect of the Japanese cultural tradition of homosexuality is its disappearance! This phenomenon is often erroneously considered to be the result of the influence of a Christianity newly re-imported since the Meiji restoration.

It is true that throughout the Meiji era (1868-1912), Protestant ministers and intellectuals influenced by Christianity were at the head of the movement to extirpate homosexuality. In reality, however, the decline of *shudo* had already begun in the 18th century when Japan was still in the middle of its long period of voluntary seclusion. The spirit of *shudo* as a 'way' began to retreat whereas a sensualist homosexuality flourished more and more. The fact that after the end of the 18th century the *kagema* mostly dressed themselves as girls (Ill. 46), while during the Genroku period they had dressed themselves gracefully as beautiful young men, also indicates a serious degeneration of the homosexual tradition. They finally disappeared as a result of the legal prohibition twice imposed; firstly in the Tempo era (1841), and secondly immediately following the Meiji restoration. The new Meiji government, the promoter of a precipitate movement of modernisation and Westernisation, decided upon a struggle against the custom of homosexuality. The law of 1873 condemned to ninety days in prison, under the head of *keikan* (sodomy), anyone who practised homosexuality. But this

121

severe attitude was to be soon relaxed. The crime of sodomy was abolished in 1883 and replaced with 'indecent assault'; the seduction of a young person of either sex of less than 16 years of age was punished by one or two months hard labour.

Homosexuality, meanwhile, was back in fashion. The best part of the army which overthrew the *bakufu* and occupied Edo, now called Tokyo, was composed of soldiers from the province of Satsuma, the centre of a Spartan homosexuality. Homosexuality thus spread through the imperial army, which became the strongest in Asia. A European living in Tokyo at that time reported:

> In peace as in war, the Japanese soldier marches arm in arm with the friend with whom he is in an intimate relation. We can say, in fact, that in the homosexual liaison too, the old samurai spirit found exultant expression on the Manchu front (in the 1880-83 war between Japan and China), in a way that one would not have seen before 1868. Many officers have told me of scenes where a soldier in love with another had fought at the risk of his own life, rushing willingly to the deadly spot. This is not simply due to the warrior spirit and contempt for death characteristic of the Japanese soldier, but also to their passion for another soldier...[8]

Homosexuality was equally fashionable among the students of Tokyo, which caused certain journalists to compose long editorials about them. According to an article in the *Japan Daily Mail*: 'Among certain students in Ushigome and Yotsuya, two areas of Tokyo, activities whose victims are young boys rather than young girls, are now in fashion. We would not wish to draw attention to conduct so abominable, but as it is happening, it would be useless to close one's eyes to it' (2 September 1896).

Other journalists also talked about the problem: for example in the *Yomiuri shinbun* (*shinbun* meaning newspaper) of 13 July 1898, the *Eastern World* of 27 May 1899, and many others. A short article published in the *Eastern World* of 19 February 1898 is interesting: 'Male homosexuality... is so widespread among the students of Tokyo that adolescent boys cannot go out at night.'

Faced with this situation, a journalist of the *Mancho-ho* hoped that the government would take measures against 'habitual conduct of such bestiality amongst the future lawyers, officers and teachers of Japan' (18 May 1899). Two days later, an article in the *Eastern World* insisted on the necessity of introducing in Japan an article corresponding to art. 174 of the penal code of the German

46. In the 18th century, the kagema were dressed as girls. (From Hiraga Gen'nai's *Kiku no sono* ('Garden of chrysanthemums', 1789. Reproduced in Iwata's *Honcho danshoku ko*.)

empire (the 'crime against nature').

Contrary to the expectations of these journalists, the law against homosexuality was never re-established. The article of the penal code against indecent assault also revealed itself to be ineffective in the prevention of homosexuality.

However, the situation began to change again at the end of the war with Russia (1904-05). Homosexuality declined again, with great rapidity, and did not recover. Tahuro Inagaki, a homosexual and a great philosophical poet born in 1900, writes in his masterpiece, 'The Aesthetics of Adolescent-Love': 'Without our noticing it, this cultural tradition has been lost to us. It certainly long enough since the young boys' *furi-sode* was replaced by the *tsutsu-sode* (a kimono without long sleeves). When we were schoolboys, we often heard of an affair in which two students had quarrelled on account of a beautiful young boy and had ended by drawing knives. It still happened occasionally that a boy would stab with his dagger someone who had attempted to take him by force. But since the new era of Taisho (1912-26), we no longer hear of this kind of thing. The *shudo*, which had clung on to life, has now reached its end.'

By what process, lasting from the end of the 18th century to the beginning of the 20th, did *shudo* go into decline, then recover temporarily only finally to die altogether? The growth of the influence of the bourgeoisie, the continuous development of capitalism, the formation of an industrialised society: this is what is involved. A similar process took place in European countries in the 18th and 19th centuries and seems to correspond to the decline of *shudo* in Japan.

I have already remarked on the curious fact that in the development of the fine arts in Europe the male body increasingly lost its aesthetic function, and we have seen in this a process, resulting from modernisation, of the monopolisation of beauty by women. We have also alluded to the profound but hidden relationship between this process and the anti-homosexual taboo. This European phenomenon corresponds to the decline of the Japanese *shudo*. Let us go into this question more deeply.

A hypothesis on the anti-homosexual attitude of modern societies

Taking note of the curious fact that in Japan the taboo against homosexuality was established without the existence of of a legal or religious prohibition, some have argued that this taboo was a result of the Christian influence newly re-imported from the West at the time of the Meiji restoration. The problem, however, is not as simple as that. The general influence of Christianity on modern Japanese society is weak.[9] The modernisation of Japan was not the transplantation of European Christian culture, but an indigenous capitalist and industrial development which had already begun in the 18th century.

Is there then a type of taboo against homosexuality whose origin need not be looked for in the Judaeo-Christian tradition, which we may consider to be specific to modern industrialised societies? Let us attempt to illuminate the problem by considering the anti-homosexual attitude during the modernisation of European societies.

Michel Foucault's analysis

In the first volume of his *History of Sexuality*,[10] Foucault analyses the process of formation of the concept of sexual perversion, criticising what he calls the 'repression hypothesis'. According to this hypothesis, repression was born in the 17th century after hundreds of years of free expression; this coincided with the development of capitalism, because within the bourgeois order sex is only valid if it assures the reproduction of the population, reproduces labour-power and produces the form of social relations. Nonetheless, 'at the level of discourses and their domains, the phenomenon is almost the reverse.' Discourses about sex proliferate endlessly, and there has been an increasing discursive ferment ever since the 18th century. The reticences of 'Victorian puritanism' were rather a historical accident. 'They were in any event a diversion, a refinement, a tactical retreat in the great process of taking sex into discourse.' What is specific to modern societies is not that they have repressed sex, but that they have 'hunted it out' and tried to govern it through 'knowledge'; because the bourgeoisie 'has invested its future in it, in sex, supposing that it has unavoidable effects on its posterity'; the bourgeoisie 'has subordinated its soul to it, thinking it to be (the soul's) most secret and most decisive element.' So, towards the middle of the 19th century not only the 'terrible crime against nature' but also petty incidents, minor indecencies and unimportant perversions became the objects of legislation, of medical intervention, of attentive clinical observation and of every kind of theoretical elaboration. Sodomy, sadism and necrophilia became something essentially different from other forbidden acts such as adultery, incest or abduction. 'This new witch-hunt against marginal sexualities involves an incorporation of perversions and a new definition of the individual. The sodomite was a heretic, the homosexual is now a species.' The modern concept of perversion, or sexual abnormality, had been established.

4. The anti-androgyne complex, basis of the anti-homosexual attitude

Sexual perversion

Foucault's demonstration seems to confirm our idea that there might be a kind of taboo on homosexuality, an anti-homosexual attitude specific to modern societies. The 'homosexual sickness' is only one of the concepts of perversion formulated since the 18th century; Foucault would say that it is not the Christian prohibition on sodomy but the modern concept of sexual abnormality which was transplanted and established in Japan with its modernisation.

His brilliant theory does not, however, explain the following curious facts:

i) the emotional reaction of the general public of our own day is very different, depending on the sex of the 'pervert';

ii) male homosexuality is always treated less tolerantly than female;

iii) a woman dressing in masculine clothing is not considered to be 'transvestite', whereas a man dressing in women's clothes is considered deviant.

An American sociologist, Deborah Feinbloom,[11] asked people to place in order of their 'degree of deviancy' the following six cases:

* a man naked in public;
* a half-naked man wearing women's underclothing in public;
* a half-naked woman wearing men's underclothing in public;
* a man completely dressed as a woman in public;
* a woman completely dressed as a man in public.

The replies obtained gave the following order of deviancy, from greatest to least:

1. the man in women's underclothing;
2. the completely naked man;
3. the man dressed as a woman;
4. the woman dressed as a man;
5. the completely naked woman;
6. the woman in men's underclothing.

What can be the significance of these extraordinary results, of this kind of 'sex discrimination'? In reality, the modern concept of perversion is not a unitary one, but rather an amalgam in which two different kinds of phenomenon are artificially combined. One inspires public aversion, anxiety and feelings of shame to a greater degree than the other. In the one, unlike the other, only men are involved. The man who loves another of his own kind, the man who dresses as a woman, and the man naked in public are the subjects of the first type. The woman who loves other women, the woman who dresses as a man, and the naked woman are subjects of the second type, together with the sadist, the voyeur and other minor perverts of either sex. The male masochist surely also falls into the first type. The public has always seen masochism on the part of a man as more abnormal and ridiculous than on the part of a woman.

What quality is inherent to the first group and causes the public's more violent reaction to it? What have men's homosexuality, transvestism and exhibitionism in common? People believe that in a homosexual relationship, one of the couple, usually the younger, plays the 'passive' role, that is to say, is regarded as 'feminine'. On seeing a man dressed as a woman, all his desires and feelings are believed to be 'feminine'. It is also believed, in our societies, that women, and only women, wish to show themselves naked.

We see here the profound taboo which lies behind our societies' anti-homosexual attitude. Modern civilisation is designed to prevent 'men' from having any qualities in common with 'woman', while the opposite is allowed, or at least treated with greater tolerance. It is this taboo, this invisible force, and not the Christian prohibition, which is the nucleus around which the system of 'sexual perversions' is organised. The idea of sexual perversion is certainly specific to modern societies, but in its strict sense is only applicable to men. The nature and function of this concept is to forbid a man to be at the same time a woman.

Certainly in psychological and psychiatric texts we find all the perversions or sexual deviations explained without reference to sex. The 'female perversions' however are only secondary concepts developed by medicine from a need for symmetry. They never inspire great aversion or panic in the general public. It's the same in the case of sadism, voyeurism and other minor male perversions. They are not regarded as incompatible with masculinity. It is permissible then to call them 'derivative or marginal perversions', so as to contrast them with what might be called the 'central perversions'. The essence of the problem is a 'taboo', that is to say the aversion, shame, mockery and anxiety experienced or shown by the public in relation to the latter, the 'central perversions'.

This invisible and amorphous taboo we may provisionally call the 'anti-androgyne complex of modern men'. This hypothesis has been developed on the basis of my own research on transvestism in Japanese society.[12]

Modern men always abandon the privilege of androgyny
Some might say that the 'anti-androgyne complex in men' has its origin in the well-known dominance of men in modern societies. However, when we look at

127

history, we see that this cannot be the case. There is plenty of evidence to show that men were not afraid to play a feminine role in ancient and oriental societies, although these societies too were organised on principles of male supremacy. This was the case for traditional Japanese society. It is difficult to find anywhere in its pre-modernisation history an explicit taboo on men dressing in women's clothes. Prince Yamato Takeru (c. 4th century AD)[13] and Minamoto no Yoshitune (1159-89,)[14] two very popular heroes, both went through various episodes of 'transvestism'. In the *no* theatre, the most refined art form of the middle ages, women's roles were played by male actors. The 17th century saw the most artistic development of transvestism: the *oyama* of the *kabuki* theatre. In general, in non-modern societies, androgyny and dressing in the clothes of the opposite sex were regarded as a privilege of the dominant sex, and not considered shameful, as they are by moderns. In fact, isn't it natural that this extraordinary privilege of also being 'the other sex' should first be given to a society's dominant sex? But what was once men's supreme advantage is now dishonour. The process of modernisation is one in which men endlessly renounce this marvellous privilege of androgyny, and eventually pass it over to women.

The anti-androgyne complex is really the 'androgyne complex'
The anti-androgyne complex, though, is at the same time really the 'androgyne complex'. This conclusion was arrived at from direct observation of the transvestite sub-culture in Japan.[12] All the transvestites interviewed had a kind of feeling which referred implicitly or explicitly to envy of women. Some said they were jealous of women because women's clothing was prettier, more varied, and today 'lighter and freer' than men's. Others showed a feeling of envy when they believed that women's life was easier because women were often permitted to depend on others. There were even some who said it was easier for them to be in the passive, i.e. 'feminine' role in sexual activity. There is no doubt that they are haunted and tormented all their lives by a feeling of jealousy.

Aren't these people just rare and extraordinary examples of 'sickness'?[15] It was suggested by a transvestite that: 'All men are like us, in their unconscious. The difference between us and the others is just the fact that we know our own feelings, and they never do.'. One cannot help but find some truth in these words. It helps to explain the extraordinarily emotional reactions (aversion, shame, mockery, anxiety etc.) of the public, and 'normal men' in particular, to transvestites who in themselves are quite inoffensive. In the unconscious of 'all' men there is always a certain resentment of women. What they see in 'perverts' with so much aversion is the external projection of their own self-image. What

128

forces them not to take on any feminine role is their repressed desire to take on certain feminine roles so as to become androgynous.[16]

The origin of the restriction on the androgyne role in modern men

The anti-androgyne and androgyne complexes produce and reinforce each other. Firstly, restriction of the androgyne role causes an envy of women to be developed in the male unconscious, which in its turn consolidates the taboo on the expression of bisexuality by means of the 'projection mechanism'. In the process of modernisation the two complexes are progressively formed and reinforce each other.

Where then does the initial restriction on modern men's androgyny or bisexuality originate? Before tackling this problem, we must first of all reconsider and re-examine the concepts of androgyny or the bisexual role, by which we moderns understand several different human phenomena. When we see a very beautiful young man, we often feel he is 'as beautiful as a young girl'. That means that we see him as a man with feminine characteristics. If we see that he is fond of make-up, jewellery and clothes, then we consider him to be effeminate. Such an attitude is not however common to all civilisations, but is specific to modern societies. Ancient Greek statues of Apollo seem to us to have an androgynous or sometimes even 'effeminate' beauty. But there is no doubt that they did not appear effeminate to the Greeks. In the time of the Valois and the Bourbons, noblemen dressed with a gaudy elegance, just like the women of their class, without being considered effeminate. It was the same in Japan. At the court of Heiankyo in the 12th century the courtiers and the young boys of their class used to powder themselves, paint on false eyelashes, perfume themselves and dress up very elegantly. This male tradition of make-up and beautiful costume was inherited by young samurai of high class and was further developed through the centuries of feudalism, becoming more and more widespread among the samurai and the middle classes as well. In the 17th century particularly, the manner of dress of the *wakashu*, young men usually between twelve and twenty years of age, became most charming and androgynous. They looked after their appearance with great care. Their hair was arranged in the *mae-gami* fashion, which was like the women's way of doing their hair. Their dress, the *furi-sode*, was often colourful and highly decorated, like that of young girls. In paintings of the period, it is often difficult to tell the sex of the characters, with their so androgynous clothing and hairstyle, unless we happen to see a sword hanging by their side. With the precipitate westernisation and modernisation, however, a sudden change took place in the dress of the *wakashu*. Men's habit of making up was completely abandoned. A haircut like that of contemporary Europeans took the place of the *mae-gami*. The *furi-sode* was no longer coloured or decorated and would be finally be replaced by the *tsutsu-sode* or by western clothing. What happened in the first years of the Meiji restoration was not so much a change but rather the total disappearance of the *wakashu* style, so much so that the word itself fell out of use.

We thus conclude that the process of modernisation, in both Japan and in Europe, involves the transformation of beauty, which had hitherto belonged to both sexes, into a specifically feminine attribute. What first of all seemed to us a restriction on men's androgyny or bisexuality is rather, in reality, a limitation or reduction of the domain of masculinity itself. It is true that Apollo was beautiful, but his beauty did not come from his 'androgynous' features; he was a beautiful *man*, in the same way as a peacock is a beautiful male.

It is not only beauty that men have lost in restricting it to women. Contemporary society, which has become liberal enough to allow women to apear nearly naked in public, continues to apply a bizarre prohibition to the exhibition of male skin. In traditional societies we find exactly the reverse. There it is women who modestly cover up the body, while male costume is generally lighter and freer. In the tradition of western art from ancient Greece onward, the nude was usually male, until this was gradually replaced by the female nude from the 16th to the 18th century. The male body thus passed from being to non-being. It is neither adorned, nor uncovered, nor looked at, nor, of course, admired. It is not only beauty but also bodily existence, or rather 'the body itself', which modern civilisation refuses to allow to men. In modern societies there is an invisible and formless power which imposes bodily existence only on women, and demands of men that they be only an active, invisible and disembodied spirit. (This, though, seems now to be beginning to change in the West.)

The de-eroticisation of the male body, a result of modernisation
It is clear then that what seemed first of all to be the restriction on androgyny and bisexuality in men is really a restriction, or rather a denaturing, of masculinity itself. We can provisionally call this process, which can also be considered as part of the general devalorisation of the male body, 'the de-eroticisation of the male body resulting from modernisation'. It is precisely in this process that we can find the most fundamental basis of the taboo on homosexuality. It is remarkable that in Japan the decline of the homosexual tradition was strictly paralleled by the phenomenon of the transfer of beauty into the exclusive possession of the world of women. In the West, the relation between these two phenomena (the taboo on

130

homosexuality and the disappearance of the aesthetic function of the male body) is more difficult to recognise because of the intervention of the well-known Christian prohibition. In any case, what society detests and abhors in homosexuality is precisely that a man offers himself to others as a beauty, as something to be looked at, as a passive object of desire. It is precisely the possibility of men's bodies having an erotic value which modern men fear and hate in this domain of the erotic.

How and why did this de-eroticisation of the male body come about during the development of civilisation? What relation does it bear to the well-known devalorisation of men's physical strength? These are difficult problems. A German ethologist, I. Eibl-Eibesfeldt,[17] describes a process which he calls the '*Vermausgrauung* of the male' (the process of making or becoming drab – 'grey as a mouse'):

> In small human communities there is nothing to fear even if everyone goes out every day dressed in a military fashion. Men can wander about, arms in hand, with animals' teeth around their necks, feathers about the head, trying to look aggressive and imposing (p. 253).
>
> It's not at all the same in an anonymous crowd. All these imposing behaviours provoke aggression in others which is not moderated by personal acquaintance. They gravely disturb communal life, and to avoid this, man conforms to mass society by depriving himself of virile and imposing displays. We see in all civilisations a process of *Vermausgrauung* of the men. Their dress becomes simple, masculine jewellery is reduced and arms are completely abandoned... The less one is noticed, the better it is.

On the other hand, 'Women live with the force display, so they escape this development.' As imposing display and eroticism are very closely related from the ethological point of view,[18] Eibl-Eibesfeldt's theory illuminates some aspects of the process of de-eroticisation of the male body, but it is not enough to explain everything.

It will be necessary to consider more generally men's 'mode of being' in modern civilisation. Here it will be enough to analyse one of the factors which seems the most important: the change from 'being' to 'having'. In traditional societies one regarded oneself as being, while in the modern, one sees oneself as having. A man was born prince, noble or official, and this he was by birth. Nothing could essentially change what he was. In modern societies, on the other hand, a man is

131

bourgeois by owning property, and becomes proletarian by losing it. 'In the latter, he is what he has, whereas in the former, he is what he is.'. It is the same for beauty. Unlike the nobles, who had always to be more beautiful than the common people, the bourgeois have no need of being beautiful themselves. They relate themselves to beauty by 'having' a beautiful woman. They are what they possess. Why would they need to be beautiful themselves? In European countries, the capitalist development of the 16th to 18th centuries ran strictly parallel to the process which Eibl-Eibesfeldt calls the '*Vermausgrauung* of the male' and which we have called the monopolisation of beauty by women; the victory of the sans-culottes is an important index of the advance of this process in Europe. The eroticism of modern societies takes the form of an eroticism of possession. Modern men continuously deprive their own body of beauty, of aesthetic function, in sum, of erotic value, so as to impose this on women, finally to regain it by 'having' a beautiful woman.

This de-eroticisation of the male body, and its most serious consequence, the formation of the anti-androgyne complex, is for men the tragedy of our civilisation. In fact, according to modern work in genetics and embryology, the development of the foetus with XY chromosomes into a normal boy involves a more complicated process than the growth of an XX foetus into a normal girl. All the primitive sexed structures of the foetus, whether it is XX or XY, have a natural tendency to differentiate and develop into female organs. If certain substances or controlling hormones are not properly supplied throughout the process of sexual differentiation, the XY foetus cannot differentiate itself as male and is therefore feminised; for the differentiation of the XX foetus as female, however, nothing needs to be provided. The 'natural' type of the brain itself is female. It is only the operation of the androgen hormone during a critical period, the sixth week after conception, which enables the differentiation of the male type of brain. According to J. Money, 'there is no doubt that nature's first inclination is to create woman.'[19] The greater difficulty in producing a male also obtains in the psychological differentiation of the sexes. The number of those who have acquired the gender-identity of the other sex (transexuals) is much higher in men than in women (a ratio of 8 to 1).[20] More social reinforcement is therefore needed for the newborn infant to become a man rather than a woman. Simone de Beauvoir wrote four decades ago that, 'One is not born a woman: one becomes one.' Subsequent new discoveries in medicine now oblige us to say likewise, 'One is not born a man: one becomes one.'

So, contrary to widespread popular opinion, the scientific discoveries of our own day seem more and more to indicate that man is an altered form of woman, and that he has in consequence a profound tendency to remain a woman. The man is a more androgynous being than the woman; this explains why in ancient civilisations the right to dress in the clothes of the opposite sex and the institutionalisation of homosexual behaviour were often accorded only to men. Unconscious wisdom had tacitly discovered the secret that the man has a stronger need to be androgynous than the woman. Having abandoned this precious wisdom, the modern spirit has invented the concept of sexual perversion and produced a society stood on its head: one where men, more fundamentally bisexual than women, are nonetheless more severely punished when they realise their androgyny and bisexuality.

The anti-homosexual attitude of society today thus has deep roots in our modern civilisation. We have been able to see, in Japan, how it was formed by a process of de-eroticisation of the male body. In the countries of Europe, this common factor is amalgamated with the traditional Christian taboo. One cannot think about the homosexual and the anti-homosexual phenomena of our society in isolation from the entire process of modernisation. Today, however, the taboo has been shaken, and is everywhere becoming weaker. This shows that modern civilisation is at a turning point.

The time has come for a serious and thorough re-examination of the modern concept of masculinity based on the total negation of bisexuality and androgyny. To re-establish masculinity on the broadest and most solid foundation, it would be useful to study the morality and aesthetics of the men of forgotten traditions such as those of the East or of ancient Greece, so as to discover their profound and hidden meaning.

Some signs of the renaissance of the *shudo* spirit
It is already twenty years since the first homosexual magazine appeared in Japan under the title *Bara-zoku* (literally 'people, *zoku*, of the rose, *bara*). Today there are four for gay men and one for lesbians. Print runs vary from thirty to fifty thousand. The homosexual world is in perpetual evolution, with the magazines acting as a sort of 'central nervous system', despite the fact that nearly all Japanese homosexuals are still obliged to hide their sexual orientation.

There is in Japan, however, no gay movement professing a clear ideology such as exists in the United States and in the countries of Europe. This is no doubt due to the fact that in Japan there have never been legal problems for homosexuals, apart from during a few years of the Meiji period. In any event, Japanese society seems to be evolving, little by little, towards a more tolerant and liberal attitude.

The work of Taruho Inagaki, poet and philosopher of adolescent-love, is today well received by many young people. In Osaka, then in Tokyo, certain cinemas which show only homosexual films have succeeded in getting a good audience, including a number of 'normal' young girls. It is particularly interesting that certain strip-cartoons showing idealised love between young men are enjoying a great popularity, especially among girls. There are a significant number of young Japanese women who are interested in both male and female homosexuality. They believe, amusingly, that all homosexual men are as beautiful as the young men in the cartoons. These innocent admirers of the homosexual man even have their own magazines (*Shosetsu June*, which provided some of the illustrations for this book, is one of them). Are these signs of a renaissance of *shudo*? Unhappily, no. There are, in fact, certain fundamental differences between *shudo* and present-day homosexuality which itself has many points in common with that of Western countries. First of all, there were in *shudo* as in Greek *paiderastia*, 'stages of development' considered to be natural, and even more or less obligatory; while the young man had the *mae-gami* he was the 'passive' object of the love of older men; when he had reached adulthood, he had to become a 'boy-lover', and sooner or later he ended up happily married. It is difficult to see these stages in contemporary homosexuality, however, and relations between adults are the dominant trend of our own day.

Another fundamental difference is that the homosexuality of *shudo* was in reality a bisexuality; as love-objects, the youths had a psychological value similar to that of girls (dress, hair-style, make-up). The *wakashu* were not young 'men' but young androgynes, one might say. Today, on the other hand, we see a good number of exclusive homosexuals who throughout their lives love not the adolescent with his androgynous beauty, but only 'men'.

We could put it, rather schematically, that modern homosexuality is that of homosexuals as a minority, whereas *shudo* was available to all, in so far as it was well integrated into the heterosexual society. This explains why in the present day homosexuality is merely tolerated, while *shudo* was both value and model.

Has the homosexual tradition any possibility of being revived as a positive value, rather than as simply an object of tolerance? This hope should not be abandoned. The flourishing of a 'homosexuality for all men', such as those of classical Japan or ancient Greece, is not incompatible with the general psychosexual development of the human being. Taking the passive role as the loved one, then becoming a lover of young men before finally integrating with the institution of heterosexuality, is an evolution which corresponds precisely to the Freudian pattern of psycho-sexual development: narcissism, homosexuality and heterosexuality. To the extent that this correspondence exists and that our androgyny can only be realised in this development, *shudo* need not be a dead idea, but will always remain an ideal.

Homosexuality should not remain a ghetto for a minority. Lesbians have played a great role in the women's liberation movement, that is to say, in relation to 'all women'. Male homosexuality, too, will be an essential catalyst in the development of 'all men', helping in the re-eroticisation of the male body, a problem of our future civilisation. According to one of my European friends, this is already taking place in the West.

137

139

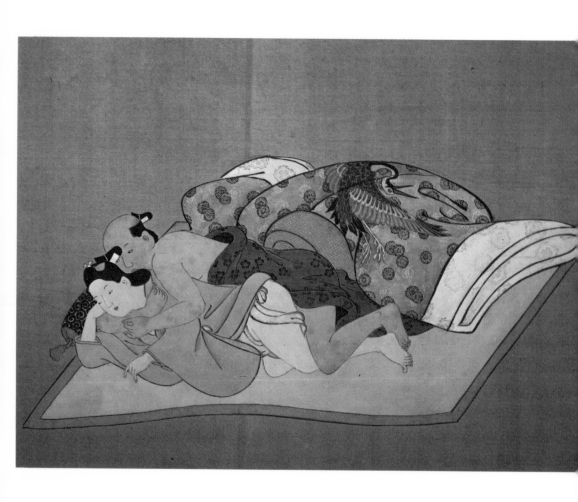

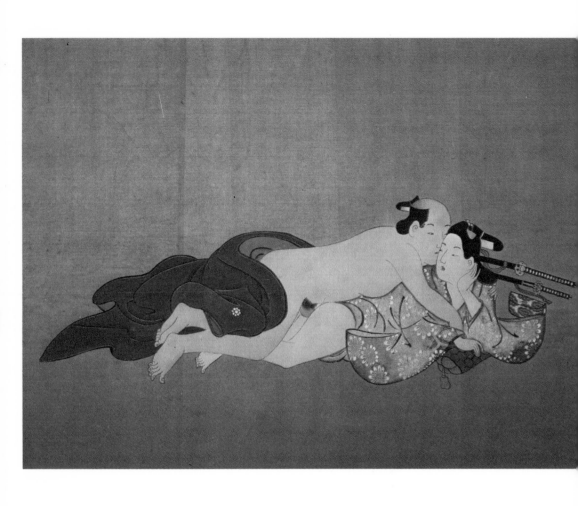

1. Chronology

Periods and dates	Events
Jo-Dai	
556	Introduction of Buddhism.
645	Consolidation of the power of the family of the Tenno and destruction of their opponents, the Soga clan.
Nara	
710	The imperial capital established at Nara.
712	*Koji ki*, the earliest Japanese text to be preserved.
Heian	
794	Capital established at Heiankyo (Kyoto).
804	Saicho's and Kukai's travels in China.
858	The Fujiwara regency established.
early 11th c.	Murasaki Shikibu writes *The Tale of Genji*.
1072-1156	'In-Sei': period of administration by the ex-emperor.
1159	Supremacy of the military clan of the Taira at the court of Heiankyo.
1184	Destruction of the Taira.
Kamakura	
1192	Minamoto no Yoritomo becomes shogun; beginning of the first *bakufu* – the *bakufu* of Kamakura.
1205	*Shin kokin shu*, anthology of poetry whose aesthetic ideal is the *yugen*.
early 13th c.	*Heike monogatari*, an epic of the fall of the Taira, from which came many subjects for the *no* theatre.
1274-81	Mongol invasions.
1333	Fall of the Kamakura.

Muromachi

1336	Ashikaga Takauji becomes shogun and makes his headquarters at Muromachi, Kyoto.
1336-92	War between Tenno courts of north and south.
1368-77	Culture protected by shogun Yoshimitsu.
15th c.	Intermittent civil war in many regions.
1467-77	Great Onin civil war at Kyoto.
late 15th c.	Period of *Sengoku*, 'Struggle between the provinces'.
1542	Arrival of the Portuguese on the island of Tanegashima.

Azuchi-Momoyama

1573	Last Ashikaga shogun deposed by Oda Nobunaga.
1582	Death of Oda Nobunaga.
1587	Beginning of Toyotomi Hideyoshi's anti-Christian policy.
1590	Hideyoshi unifies Japan.
1598	Death of Hideyoshi.
1600	Battle of Sekigahara, victory of Tokugawa Ieyasu.

Edo

1603	Establishment of Tokugawa shogunate (*bakufu* of Edo).
1613	Total prohibition of Christianity.
1636	*Sa-koku*, the closure of the country.
1688-1703	Genroku culture: Basho, Saikaku and Chikamatsu.
1803-30	Bunka-Bunsei culture: Utamaro, Hokusai and Hiroshige.
1841-43	Reform policy of Tempo era.
1854	'Opening of the country' forced by Commodore Perry.
1867-68	Fall of the Tokugawa *bakufu*, restoration of imperial power (Meiji restoration).

2. Map of Japan

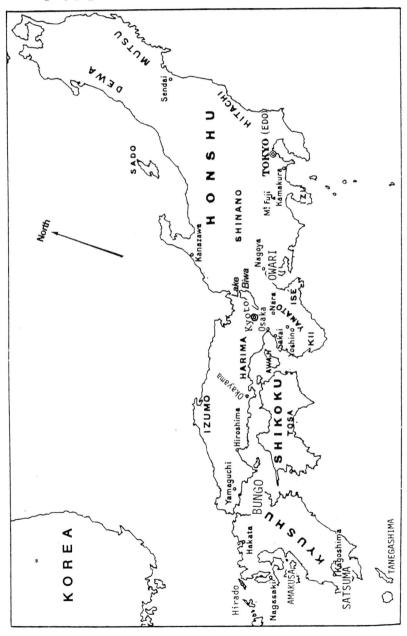

3. Notes

Notes to Introduction

1. *Danshoku bunken shoshi*, Sadao Iwata , Toba, 1977.
2. 'Man, modernity and the homosexual taboo' (in Japanese), *Research Report of Kochi University*, vol. 29, 121-147, 1980.
3. 'Une hypothèse sur l'attitude anti-homosexuelle spécifique aux sociétés modernes', *Research Report of Kochi University*, vol. 30, 9-12, 1981 and vol. 31, 63-68, 1982.
4. Bon, M., *Développment personnel et l'homosexualité*, Epi, Paris, 1975. Bon, M. and D'Arc, A., *Rapport sur l'homosexualité de l'homme*, Éditions Universitaires, 1974.

Notes to Chapter One

1. 'Nippon' is the correct name for Japan.
2. Luis Frois, *Historia do Japão*, ch. 1. (German translation, *Die Geschichte Japans* by G. Schurhammer and E. A. Voretzsche, Verlag Asia Major, 1926).
3. Cited by J. Monsterleet in his *L'église du Japon*, 1958, p. 132.
4. Schurhammer, G. and Wicki, J., *Epistolae S. Francisci Xavierii aliaque eius scripta*, 1945 (Japanese translation by P. Arpe and I. Inoue, 1949).
5. Frois, op. cit., ch. 3.
6 ibid., ch. 16. Fr. Belchoir arrived in Japan in 1556.
7. ibid., ch. 83.
8. *Sumario de las cosas que pertenecen a la Provincia de Japon y al govierno della compuesto por el Padre Alexandro Valegnani, Visitador de las Indias de Oriente, dirigido a N. P. General Claudio Aquaviva*, ch. 1. (Japanese translation by T. Matsuda and T. Sakuma as *Nippon Ju'nsatsu ki*, Togensha, Tokyo, 1965.)
9. This is not an unreasonable hypothesis, because the three sons of Oda Nobunaga were all very welcoming to Catholic teachings and missionaries.
10. Storry, R. and Foreman, W., *The Samurai*. (French translation by J. Maillot, *Les samourais*, Éditions Atlas, 1978.)

Notes to Chapter Two

1. That is to say, Kukai as a mysterious pilgrim.
2. Kukai's posthumous title.
3. Literally 'Japanese chronicles continued', of the year 797.
4. *Ji* = servant, *do* = child.
5. A scholar of Japanese literature who lived in the Edo period.
6. Literally 'Japanese chronicles', appeared in 720.
7. A half-legendary Japanese empress of the 3rd century.
8. Although the meaning of *uruwashiki* (beautiful, graceful) *tomo* (friend), here rendered as 'very intimate friends' is no longer clear to us moderns, there is no doubt that Amano Hafuri and Shinu no Hafuri were a homosexual couple. But, contrary to the opinion of Mr Iwata, it seems to me that the sin of *azunai* refers to the burial together of two priests who were under a duty each exclusively to serve his own god. We thus have no evidence of a taboo against homosexuality in Japan's distant past.
9. According to a pamphlet distributed to pilgrims at Mount Koya, cited by F. Toussaint in his *Histoire du Japon*, Fayard, 1969.
10. Shiba Ryotaro, *Scenes of Kukai's life*, Shincho-sha, Tokyo, 1974.
11. After Saicho, all these divinities were honoured as the guardians of the Tendai school.
12. See *The Tale of Genji*, tr. R. Shiffert, Orient Fr., p. 106 ff.

Notes to Chapter Three

1. Yagoro was Mochisada's name before he reached adulthood. This custom of changing the name at coming-of-age is particularly found amongst men of high class.
2. After the death of Hideyoshi, he fought against Tokugawa Ieyasu for the Toyotomi. He lost the battle of Sekigahara, where he was killed.
3. Mount Hiei was a holy place forbidden to women.
4. To reduce the suffering of the condemned man, it was usual to attend the *harakiri* and cut off his head.

Notes to Chapter Four

1. One can read in Mishima's *The Golden Pavilion* how this jewel of Japanese architecture was utterly destroyed by an arson attack.
2. It is impossible to provide an exact translation for *yugen*, but Sieffert has rendered it by 'subtle charm'. (See Zeami, *La tradition secrète du Nô*, translated and with commentary by R. Sieffert, Gallimard, Paris, 1960.)
3. In Iwata's 'Bibliography of homosexuality', we find seventeen *no* plays.
4. Ariwara no Narihira (825-880). Poet, and hero of the 'Story of Ise'. His name is synonymous with masculine beauty.
5. 'Tears of blood' denotes extreme distress.
6. Some stories may be read in French in *Contes d'amour des samourais* by Ihara Saikaku, tr. K. Kato, Jacques Damase, 1981.
7. Thevénot, *Relations de divers voyages curieux, qui n'ont point été I publiées...*, André Praland, Paris, 1664.
8. This article was first published in 1933. Nowadays a male prostitute is called *dan-sho* (*dan* = male, etc.) or a 'gay-boy'.
9. 1867-1941, an ethnographer and botanist. His correspondence with J. Iwata is a mine of information on the history of Japanese homosexuality.
10. The pilgrimage to the great Shinto temple of Ise was fashionable during the Edo period.
11. 1728-79. A scholar who employed his talents in different fields of science, and known too as the author of works of science fiction.
12. The best-known area of homosexual brothels in Edo.

Notes to Chapter Five

1. *Jakudo*: the way (*do*) of the young (*jaku*). Another name for *shudo*.
2. *O-wakashu*: an older *wakashu*. A young man who keeps his *mae-gami* even after reaching adulthood.
3. An anonymous work.
4. *Giri* is difficult to translate. According to Ceselin's French-Japanese Dictionary (1940): 1. Strict moral obligation arising from some kind of tie. 2. Proper behaviour, external forms of behaviour to be followed so as not to lose face.
5. Literally: he (*ja*) who feels love (*nen*).
6. Ihara Saikaku, *Cinq amoureuses*, tr. G. Bonmarchand, Gallimard.

7. Satsuma was famous throughout the whole country for its homosexual customs. This was explained by the martial character of its population. Raised in a Spartan fashion, they disdained women. At war, they found satisfaction in their comrades in arms.

8. Cited in *Das Geschlechtsleben in Glauben, Sitte, Brauch und Gewohnheitsrecht der Japaner* by Friedrich S. Krauss, Leipzig, 1910.

9. In 1943, 75 years after the Meiji restoration, there were 320,000 Christians (only 0.3% of the total population of Japan), while in 1595, 48 years after the arrival of Francis Xavier, there were 300,000 converts (2.2% of the population at that time).

10. *History of Sexuality*, Volume One.

11. Seymour Lawrence, *Transvestites and Transsexuals: Mixed Views*, Delacorte Press, 1976.

12. Watanabe, T., 'A study of the Japanese transvestite culture, with some considerations on the deeper causes of the taboo on men's dressing in women's clothing' (in Japanese), *Research Report of Kochi University*, vol. 29, 127-147, 1980.

13. A legendary prince, disliked by his father emperor Keiko, spent his life in travels and military expeditions. He sometimes dressed as a woman so as to assassinate enemy chiefs.

14. A military chief, hated by his brother the shogun Yoritomo, tragically spent his life as a fugitive perpetually travelling. He was skilled in dressing as a woman to escape the vigilance of his enemies.

15. In his exhaustive investigation of transvestism, H. Brierley says: 'Nothing indicates that transvestism itself should be regarded as an illness or neurosis, if by these terms we mean a serious deterioration of an individual's manner of living. On the contrary, it would seem that the available evidence lends weight to the hypothesis that transvestism is associated with persons who are capable and competent, rather than otherwise.' (*Transvestism: A Handbook with Case Studies for Psychologists, Psychiatrists and Counsellors*, Pergamon Press, Oxford, 1979.)

16. The 'androgyne complex' may be related to Jung's 'anima'. But this complex refers principally to the desire to be a woman developed in the male unconscious as a result of the repression of the anima. This complex, as well as the 'anti-androgyne complex', is specific to the men of modern times, whereas Jung's anima is present in all men.

17. Eibl-Eibesfeldt, I., *Liebe und Hass: Zur Naturgeschichte elementare Verhaltensweisen*, Piper Verlag, Munich, 1970.

18. Lorentz, K., *Das sogennante Böse; Zur Naturgeschichte der Agression*, Borotha Schöler Verlag, Vienna, 1963. (English edition: *On Aggression.*)
19. Money, J., 'Determinants of Human Gender Identity Roles', in Money, J. and Musaph, H., *Handbook of Sexology*, Elsevier, 1977, pp. 57-80.
20. Benjamin, H., *The Transsexual Phenomenon*, Warner Books, New York, 1966.

4. Glossary

Amida. Buddha of the West (in Sanskrit, Amitabha), the object of a particular cult in the Ikko sect.

Ashigaru. Light infantry with two swords, the lowest rank in the samurai hierarchy.

Bakufu. Government of the shoguns, who effectively ruled Japan from 1186 to 1867, acting as guardians of the Tenno.

Bosatsu. Bodhisattva (an enlightened one who has vowed not to rest in Nirvana while there are beings not yet saved).

Buke, Bushi. Samurai (*bu* = arts of war, *ke* = family, *shi* = gentleman).

Bushido. Way and code of the samurai.

Butsu. Buddha.

Chigo. Young boy, then (sexual) favourite, especially a priest's.

Choji. Vegetable oil.

Dan-sho. Modern male prostitute (*dan* = male).

Daimyo. Provincial lord (*dai* = great, *myo* = name).

Daishi. Great (*dai*) master (*shi*).

Dengaku. Ancient dance accompanied by music, comic pantomime of Buddhist origin.

Deva (Sanskrit). The gods who protect Buddhism. In Japanese, *ten.*

Do. Way, the Chinese Tao.

Emakimono. Painting (*e*) in a roll (*makimono* = something rolled).

Ennen-no-mai. Dances performed in the Buddhist monasteries of the middle ages (*ennen* = longevity, *mai* = dance).

Furi-sode. Long sleeves of the kimono, then the long-sleeved kimono worn by women and boys.

Geisha. A skilled performer whose task was to enliven feasts with songs and dances.

Giri. Obligation, duty.

Haiku. Short poem.

Happi. Worker's short jacket.

Harakiri. Literally to cut (*kiri*) the belly (*hara*), the favoured form of suicide among the samurai.

Harikata. Dildo.

Hatchiman Daibosatsu. God of warriors.

Iki. Chic, elegant.

155

In-sei. Administration (*sei*) of a retired emperor (*in*).
Iroko. Male prostitute (*iro* = erotic, *ko* = boy).
Jaku-do. Way of the young (*jaku* = young).
Ji-do. Young page or young girl attendant.
Ju-do. Judo, the way of suppleness.
Kabuki. Popular drama which had a great success during the 17th and 18th centuries.
Kaburo. Woman prostitute's little servant-girl.
Kage-ko. Male prostitute (*kage* = shade).
Kagema. As *kage-ko* (*ma* = room).
Kamishimo. Ceremonial costume of the samurai.
Kana. Phonetic writing.
Kannon. Bodhisattva Avalokiteshvara.
Kashiki. Young male dancer and prostitute.
Keikan. Sodomy.
Kimono. Long full-skirted robe worn in Japan by both sexes.
Kirishitan. Christian.
Ko-domo. Child.
Koi. Love.
Kongo. Something very pure, diamond, then, an actor's servant.
Koto. 13-stringed zither.
Kosode. White under-shirt (literally, little (*ko*) sleeve (*sode*).
Kyu-do. Way of archery (*kyu* = bow).
Kyogen. Short farce performed as an interlude between *no* plays.
Mae-gami. Hair (*gami*) at the front (*mae*), locks of hair at the forehead.
Maitreya (Sanskrit). The next Buddha, who will appear on earth 5,670,000,000 years after the Buddha Çakyamouni. In Japanese: Miroku.
Mie. Outward honour, vanity.
Monogatari. Story, novel (*mono* = thing, *gatari* = narrative).
Nanshoku (or *danshoku*). Homosexuality (*nan* = male, *shoku* = eroticism).
Nasake. Sympathy, compassion.
Nen. Feeling.
Nenja. Man who loves *wakashu*. (*Ja* = he).
No. Lyric drama of the middle ages, in which the actor of the principal role wears a mask.
O-wakashu. Older (*o*) *wakashu*, a young man who still keeps the *mae-gami* after reaching adulthood.
O-kosho. Young page.

Onna. Woman.

On'nagata. Male actor who plays women's roles.

Oyama. As *On'nagata.*

Rishu-Kyo. Prajnaparamita sutra, 'On the Highest Wisdom', one of the fundamental texts of the Mahayana Buddhist canon (Sanskrit *prajna* = wisdom, *paramita* = perfection).

Sa-do. Way of Tea.

Sake. Alcoholic spirit made from rice.

Samurai. Member of the warrior class.

Sarugaku. Dance of the monkeys (*saru*), ancestor of *no.*

Shamisen. Traditional Japanese three-stringed guitar.

Shaka. Buddha Çakyamouni.

Shingon. True speech, name of the school of esoteric Buddhism introduced from China in 806 by Kukai.

Shinto. Way (*to*) of the gods (*shin*), indigenous religion of Japan before the introduction of Buddhism.

Sho-do. Way of calligraphy.

Sho. Prostitute.

Shogun. 'Great general', title of the head of the samurai class. See *bakufu.*

Shonin (or *shonen*). Literally, young (*sho*) person (*nin*), i.e. a boy.

Shu-do. Way of (male) adolescents.

Shunga. Pornographic painting.

So-hei. Soldier (*hei*) monk (*so*).

Soshi. Pamphlet, notebook, then memoirs, book, tale.

Tateyaku. Male role in *kabuki.*

Tendai. Mount Tiandai in China. Name of the Buddhist philosophy introduced from China in 805 by Saicho.

Tengu. Legendary mountain creatures with long noses and wings.

Tenno. Emperor of Japan (*ten* = heaven).

Tobi-ko. A low class of male prostitute.

Torimochi. Interposition, intervention, reception.

Tsu-jin. Man of the world, elegant person (*tsu* = worldly knowledge).

Ukiyo-e. Popular art which depicts what one sees in everyday life. (*E* = painting, *ukiyo* = this world).

Uruwashiki tomo. Very intimate friend (*uruwashiki* = beautiful, graceful).

Wakashu. (Male) adolescent. Originally, young (*waka*) people (*shu*).

Yaro. Peasant (*ya-ro* = country-man), then actor-prostitute.

Yamabushi. Literally one who sleeps (*bushi*) on the mountain (*yama*); a hermit who practices austerity in living upon a mountain.
Yugen. Literally, subtle (*yu*) and profound (*gen*), subtle charm.
Zen. Meditation, in Sanskrit *dhyana*. A school of Buddhism which substitutes contemplation for the search for truth through the holy writing.
Zoku. People.

GMP books can be ordered from any bookshop in the UK, and from specialised bookshops overseas. If you prefer to order by mail, a comprehensive catalogue is available on request, from:
GMP Publishers Ltd (GB), P O Box 247, London N17 9QR.

In North America order from Alyson Publications Inc, 40 Plympton St, Boston MA 02118, USA.

Name and Address in block letters please:

Name _____

Address _____

_____

_____